International Best-seller

How to COMMUNICATE *with* Anyone

Revised for 2021

Change the way you interact with people forever

DAVID HIRST

***HOW TO COMMUNICATE WITH ANYONE**

Cover Design 2021 by Chu Lee Shen
ISBN 13: 978-983-3832-25-5

First published in 2011 by Advantage Quest Publications edition issued by arrangement with the author. Seventh imprint 2015. Revised by the author in 2021 for online publication only.

Advantage Quest Publications is an imprint of Advantage Quest Sdn. Bhd. (320311-T)

For information regarding the 2021 online publication, contact the author directly at davidjhirst@yahoo.co.uk

Print version (2015) Distributed in Singapore exclusively by Advantage Quest Pte. Ltd. 200905563N)

Printed in Malaysia by Printmate Sdn. Bhd. (89371-D) 14 & 16, Jalan Industri P.B.P. 7, Taman Industri Pusat Bandar Puchong, 47100 Puchong, Selangor D.E.

CONTENTS

Communication: it's a choice

> **'The most important things are the hardest to say, because words diminish them.'**
>
> *Stephen King*

Communication, at best, can be an enjoyable, informative and fun-filled event. On the other hand, at worst, it is balancing on the perilous ledge of a linguistic chasm at the interface of pain and suffering; the nightmare from hell that would make cutting off one of your own limbs a veritable pleasure compared with entering into certain interactions. In simple terms, it can be a delight or torture. And it's complicated because of the variety of Englishes that exist out there in the real world. Let me give you an example of what I mean.

"Hellohw. "
"I'd like to put my car in for a service please."
"Ah, yes when you want put your car for service? "
"This afternoon?"
"Cannot."
"Tomorrow?"
"Cannot."
"The day after tomorrow?" "Cannot."
"Well, when can I service the car then?"
"Next week Monday 10am can."
"Okay, then. Next Monday it is."
"Your name is Mr. Again?"
"No my name is not Mr. Again."
"Aaah you are Mr?"

> *"Yes, I am a Mister."*
> *"Hmph. I cannot service you unless you give your name. What's your name prease?"*
> *"David Hirst."*
> *"Mr. David."*
> *"No, Mr Hirst."*
> *"Aah Mr. Hiss. And you are from?"*
> *"?... Planet Earth* (getting irritated)."
> *"Huh? No. You are from which company?"*
> *"Hirst Development and Training Services."*
> *"Huh? Hiss Develop Train Service. Okay."*
> *"And you are?"*
> *"Er...A human being...?"*
> *"Huh? You are your company."*
> *"Yes, I am my company."*
> *"Oh! You have phone number."*
> *"Yes, I have a phone number thank you* (very irritated at this stage)."
> *"Haiyah! Wot your phone number?"* .... And so on...

Of course, if I had more sense, I'd not be so sarcastic and the exchange would have probably been different. If I had been more communicative the above interaction would have gone a lot smoother. Certainly, things would have been better with a little more understanding from the other person's perspective, but good communication actually requires so much more than this.

It's not so much about the quality of English that you have, although it certainly helps to have a good command of the language, it is how you handle things when the transfer of information breaks down. Then the true quality of your communication skills shines through. This is particularly the case during this time of Covid 19 when face-to-face contact is reduced to the level of online meetings.

This book is designed to give the reader a comprehensive guide to communicating in a wide variety of situations to help avoid communication breakdown. It also gives easy-to-follow **Golden Guidelines** to help navigate your way through the labyrinth of today's fast-changing, technology-driven world.

We are at war. A little dramatic I grant you, but we are constantly at war with ourselves and others as we battle our way through the maze of what it is to communicate in business and social settings in multi-lingual societies. But there is a way out, and that's to understand a little more about why people act the way they do and respond more effectively with our communication. In the following chapters there is a wealth of information to help you recognize when people are struggling with the information you are giving them, even though they won't admit it, and to be aware of the different ways of putting your message across more effectively.

At the time of writing, this book is pretty much the only guide you'll ever need to navigate your way around social and business communities. Yes, good English helps, but then nearly all the information contained here can be applied to any language. In particular, there is as much emphasis on the messages that are not said, as the messages that are. Body language is dealt with in some depth as is emotional and social intelligence, which are themes that run throughout the various chapters. There is down-to-earth practical advice as well as information to make you think and reflect on recent interactions, which will help you in your future ones. It's not a magic wand that can transform you into a master communicator, but if you follow all the advice given, it will take you pretty close.

I hope you enjoy the writing style as it contains a considerable amount of dry, tongue-in-cheek humour, and a big spoonful of irreverence. Life is just too short to take everything too seriously, don't you think?

To communicate with literally anyone requires the understanding of a number of distinct skill-sets that help not just with communication but the quality of life you strive for. So, for my part I've tried to write an entertaining and informative message. Your task is to make one of those difficult decisions that could potentially change your life, and that's to turn to the next page, or not. So the challenge is on, and it's a choice. To communicate with anyone is also a choice.

> **'The biggest and most profitable investment you can ever make is in yourself.'**
>
> ***David Hirst***

1. First Impressions – Face-to-Face: the make or break of a relationship

'It is only at the first encounter that a face makes its full impression on us.'

Arthur Schopenhauer

There's an interesting paradox which goes "first impressions are so important, yet most people get them terribly wrong." At this time of Covid, do you make a fist bump, an elbow bump or a Kung-fu salute? What if someone comes at you with a fist bump and you, quite rightly, don't think physical contact is a good idea? The answer is fairly straightforward unless you want to complicate matters. In business, you follow the lead of the "buyer" ("sellers" - idea or product - are always subordinate to buyers). In other words, you match whatever they do (and keep some hand sanitizer nearby to use discreetly). And if they do nothing, then you match that too and continue with some small talk.

In social situations you can take a similar approach or lead. The stakes are (generally) lower. And still remember to sanitise regularly. By the time you read this, we may have all been vaccinated and we can go about our lives in a similar way to before. Things will never be exactly the same. In the future, handshakes will become less common, even with face-to-face interactions, and there will be more online interactions, particularly among younger entrepreneurs.

However, there will still be a need to get the handshake right. And so many people don't.

The most common mistakes are offering something slimy that you might find more suited to a wet market, or what feels more like a freshly killed pigeon instead of a hand to shake. In some cases, people like to crush the hand of the person they are meeting in the misguided belief that it shows extra sincerity. What it actually does is serve one purpose, which is to confirm the belief that there is life on other planets, because for sure they can't be from this one. And then you have the complete horse's bottom of a person who insists on turning your hand anti-clockwise as they grip it to indicate that they see themselves as superior and are intent on controlling the conversation (I'll cover this in detail in the Body Language section).

Then we get to the shake. First, there are people who just don't want to let go; they just keep shaking and shaking. There must be some sort of rational explanation for this such as wanting to show that they really, really like the other person, or perhaps they have been living in a cave for the past twenty years.

Another group of people are those people that need to use both hands or touch the other person's elbow with their other hand. While this may be acceptable in a friend-to-friend greeting, it's much less acceptable in a business setting.

The 'dead pigeon' hand type of person will often not shake at all and just leave their hand there for you to do something with. Not only does this feel awful, it might indicate that you just cannot be bothered with the person you are shaking hands with.

So, what should you do?

The hand extends until the web between the thumb and forefinger meets the same from the other person. The grip should be firm without crushing. Shake two to four times and then let go. This should send a signal to the other person to let go too. Likewise, if you feel the other side let go earlier, you do the same. It's really as simple as that.

If you are one of those people who are prone to palmer sweating, one thing to remember is to carry a tissue in your pocket and ensure your hand is as dry as possible. Similarly, if you are carrying a cold drink make sure you either hold it in your left hand or hold it with a serviette. Common sense really.

I remember once when a Dutch friend of mine, who was posted to Malaysia, came up to me at a wedding reception there and asked me to shake his hand. A little odd, I thought, but did as I was asked. He then asked me if he had a sweaty palm. I replied that he hadn't. He then told me that he had just shaken a man's hand and the other person had wiped his hand on the front of his shirt. I explained that Malays will often bring their hand to their chest (heart) after shaking hands as it's a cultural symbol of friendliness: no need for alarm. Cultural differences count.

Incidentally, some Muslim ladies may prefer not to shake hands with men (and vice versa): some do and some don't, it depends on several factors. The best advice here is to wait to see if they offer their hand first. This way you can be assured of avoiding any potentially embarrassing event.

After the initial greeting, people who are less confident usually do one of two things. The first is that they hurriedly fumble for their name card (if they have one on them at the time) which they proffer at the earliest opportunity. It takes on the role of a security blanket. The second possibility is that they immediately plunge their hands in their pockets or lock them up behind their backs or, slightly better, in front of them. Men will often opt for the hands-in-the-pockets defence which can look very awkward, especially if they find a coin or keys there to play with.

The main issue is that the other person's subconscious is aware of what your body is doing and may then – if serious enough to warrant it – bring this to the attention of your conscious mind. The conscious mind will then make a simple and often wrong judgement that you are not worth talking to and close the conversation as quickly as possible.

The hands are an incredibly important part of communication, and if they are hidden, it sends a message that your words may also be hiding something. It's a similar case when holding your hands behind you. For sure, the person's mind will not immediately and consciously say "Ah, he's got his hands in his pocket, so he may be trying to hide the truth", but what happens is that the message that gets filtered from the subconscious to the conscious mind may result in a feeling of discomfort, or in an extreme case, hostility.

Hands really are extremely important supporters of the words you mention. So you need to show them. Cast your mind back to when you were last with your friends. Where were your hands?

I bet they weren't hidden. In fact, I suggest they were probably gesturing in front of you. It's what you do naturally when you are feeling comfortable with people. In effect, you are helping the understanding of your message.

Further, studies suggest that at a subconscious level, if hand gestures are out of synch (incongruent) with the words said, the listener will, in most cases, be influenced more by the body language than the words used.

Perhaps the worst thing someone can do is fold them in front of their chest, creating a physical barrier between them and the person they're talking to. While this may make the person folding their arms feel more secure, it has exactly the opposite effect on the other person. At an intuitive level they will feel the arm-folder is being defensive and uncooperative, and the other person will therefore react accordingly.

Another common body language action following a handshake is to reach out to a table, chair or anything else that happens to be nearby. They are, in effect, trying to hide behind the items. It is why people feel so much more comfortable speaking to an audience from behind an object such as a lectern. It acts as a castle wall to protect them from their listeners. On a sidenote, speaking in public and meeting people for the first time have a lot in common in terms of what the body language does. For example, as soon as people release the grip from shaking hands, or stand in front of an audience, they often feel as if their own hands and feet have grown in size and they don't quite know what to do with them.

This can result in ridiculous situations where less confident presenters or entrepreneurs cross their legs while standing up, almost as if they are trying to trip themselves up.

Even those who know they should keep their hands in front of them will often squeeze them so tightly together that it looks like they are trying to break their own fingers. You can literally see blotches where the blood has been cut off. And all of this makes the other person feel uneasy, which then leads to strained conversation or uncomfortable silences in the dialogue.

What you *should* do after shaking hands is to bring the (right) hand to around waist height and in front of the body. The left hand should already be there. Your elbows will have approximately a 95-degree angle, and your hands should be open. Be aware not to clasp the hands too tightly as this will signal unease. It is a good idea if your palms are facing more upwards than towards you. This avoids showing the backs of your hands, which can be seen as defensive. However, the main point is to make sure the posture feels comfortable for you. If it doesn't, you will be less focussed on what the other person is saying. And they will notice. This posture not only looks confident, it also encourages the other person to relax and feel comfortable with you too. It offers the least threatening posture for the other person. And remember to smile.

I have met many people who have been tasked with introducing themselves to people at gatherings, parties and networking events, but know that they get very nervous when they try. It's almost as if they know they should be a bit more outgoing, but are not quite sure what they should be saying and doing.

If you are comfortable with a person and you are interested in what they are saying, your body pays attention too.

Well, first you should pat yourself on the back for making the effort. Then, to feel more comfortable, you can create your own safety net by holding a pen or other small item, if it helps. Later, when you develop more confidence, you can change the item to something smaller and more unobtrusive until you can do without it altogether. However, please make sure that whatever you use makes no noise. If you have the annoying habit of clicking a pen repeatedly, it will either send the message that you are high on meth-amphetamines or that you have the confidence of a hermit crab. Be aware that fidgeting of any sort will send the message that you are uncomfortable in the other person's company and you would rather not be talking with them. Similarly, if your feet keep moving or shuffling about, it indicates that you, quite literally, want to move away from the interaction. You see, if you are comfortable with a person and you are interested in what they are saying, your body pays attention.

What you *should* do is make sure your feet are approximately two thirds of the width of your shoulders; perhaps slightly less for ladies. Have your weight fairly evenly balanced, although you may find that as you relax more with the person you're talking with, the weight shifts from one leg to the other. This is especially so for people with low blood pressure as it helps constrict the leg valves and helps the flow of blood back to the heart. If the other person also has low blood pressure an interesting thing occurs: one party will usually suggest they 'grab a seat' or similar. It is the result of the subconscious mind communicating with the conscious mind for a better interaction. You see, the power of the subconscious mind is vast and picks up on every movement. For sure, there is still much more research needed in this area to understand the complete mechanisms of exactly how the subconscious works, but we do have enough evidence to extrapolate many truths about human interaction.

Golden Guideline

Make eye contact, smile and offer a firm, but not overly strong handshake and introduce yourself.

'The happiest conversation is that of which nothing is distinctly remembered, but a general effect of pleasing impression.'

Samuel Johnson

Summary

All it takes is about 60 – 90 seconds before someone makes a preliminary judgement of you, so first impressions are crucial. They will then give you another 4 – 5 minutes to confirm or re-calibrate their initial judgement. These impressions are also very hard to undo once they've been formed.

Some of the best advice is to 'just be yourself', but that's quite difficult when it's important to make a favourable impression on someone. However, it is possible if you follow the golden guideline, and above all, be genuine and sincere. And remember to smile.

2. Social and Professional Networking Events

'The richest people in the world look for and build networks, everyone else looks for work.'

Robert Kiyosaki

Meeting People: networking

Social gatherings rarely happen out of coincidence: they are usually arranged. They could be club or society arrangements or something more formal such as attending a formal networking event. And going to these types of gatherings offers a lot of opportunity for what is referred to as building 'Golden Bridges'. The term itself comes from Sun Tzu's 'Art of War', but has been adapted to refer to reaching out to the other party, rather than just building a position to retreat to.

It should be fairly straightforward, but many people need a few pointers to avoid making a complete dog's mess of themselves.

So, what is networking and is it possible to do it without appearing to be the seller of second-hand cars? Is it at all possible to network and still be respected, and your friendship enjoyed by those whom you wish to influence? The answer is yes, but there are caveats.

There are also a few Golden Guidelines you really should observe to help you make the most of the meeting and minimise the chances of an awkward encounter.

If you shout "I won! I won!" every time you get money from an ATM machine, people will look at you strangely, to say the least. Likewise, if you turn up to any social or work gathering in attire that comes from a different decade let alone a different century, then people are going to take one look at you and move to another part of the room to avoid coming into contact with you. So, think about what other people are likely to be wearing and prepare your look with a little thought to the image you wish to project.

The objective is to stand out in a positive way and not to be remembered as the village idiot.

Giving hard and fast rules about what you should and should not wear is about as useful as ordering a diet water in a restaurant. However, there are a few strategies you can follow to help reduce the chances of making a faux pas. I agree that certain colours and patterns do not go together. I also think that wearing a tie with a short-sleeved shirt does look a bit out of place. But if everyone else is doing it, then why not? Actually, I don't recommend it, but I think you get the point I'm making. Try to fit in rather than stand out. However, the way we dress for business is changing. It's becoming less formal. Ties are becoming reserved for only more formal occasions. It is not a fad. It's been happening over the past twenty to thirty years.

The following guideline is not set-in stone but to think about. By all means experiment with what you wear and see how it changes or affects your personality, and your friend's reactions. The objective is to fit in, and when you are more confident, stand out in a positive way and not to be remembered as the village idiot.

Golden Guideline 1

Always consider wearing clothing that is on a par or slightly, just slightly smarter than the type of people you wish to meet

As Coco Chanel puts it "If a person is poorly dressed you notice their dressing, but if they are impeccably dressed, you notice the person."

Fools Abound

Despite rumours to the contrary, networking is alive and well, although it has taken on a different form than the mass events held at societies and gatherings of the 2000s. It has become a lot more exclusive. People are tired of being pumped for information about themselves and who they work for. They have had enough of the facade of friendship from vultures that have 'selling' in neon lights plastered across their furrowed brows. And they're fed up of their PAs complaining bitterly about being hassled and harangued by every shallow salesman on the planet claiming to know the answer to all of life's (or your company's) problems.

I remember one such event where this particular consultant had a fold-out business card listing all his so-called business qualifications. Not only did it look tacky, archaic and ridiculous, it created an instant turn-off to the thought of any business dealings. And the card was all he had – no website, no social media account and no real understanding of the importance of an online presence. However, the card matched his personality to a tee as he came across as a person who could fix anything for a price. "Want your mother-in-law to disappear?" nudge-nudge, wink-wink. "Want to buy a second-hand car luv, no accidents honest or strike me down with a bolt of lightning." Interestingly I never saw him again, and there was a nasty storm that evening.

There was another occasion when this incredibly irritating Client Relationship Specialist introduced himself to our group and then proceeded to analyse each of our answers as if he was dissecting a frog in high school. We also learned – he stated – that he was a Neuro-linguistic Programming expert, and that he had the ability to make people do exactly what he wanted. In fact his ego knew no bounds, and neither did his body language which twisted and turned to mimic the person he was talking to. The probable reason he was doing this is related to the notion that if you are 'like-bodied,' you are 'like-minded'. And it's true that there is substantial amount of scientific evidence to suggest that if you have similar body postures and mannerisms as another person, then you are likely to think in the same way as them. This is recognised by the subconscious mind and gets filtered to the conscious mind with the result that you feel more comfortable with the other party.

Rather wickedly, two of our group decided to enjoy this so-called 'specialist' and competed to see just how ridiculous they could get him to look. They dutifully took turns to maintain the conversation and drop titbits of juicy information to keep the man interested. In turn, he brainlessly aped their movements until he actually made more than a passing resemblance to a duck playing a one-man-band without the instruments. He was about as ridiculous as a starter button on a bicycle. When it finally dawned on him that we were teasing him – and this did take some time as his ego and sense of superiority really had the better of him – he mustered what pride he had remaining and left us with a curt goodbye. "Idiot" one in our group said loud enough for nearby groups to hear. And this is precisely the risk at networking events: meeting so-called 'specialists' like the one we did. And far from them being a rarity, they have cropped up at nearly every gathering I've been invited to.

Golden Guideline 2

If you are invited to a networking event and are charged with the task of identifying potential clients or similar, remember to be as genuine (and tactful) as possible.

Certainly, you should never point out that the other person has overdone it with the garlic, and their chances of getting a result with the attractive MC are about as likely as the Dodo suddenly resurfacing in a garden pond. However, you should be genuine about trying to find something in common with the other person. But don't force it. As Fredrich Nietzsche puts it "To use the same words is not a sufficient guarantee of understanding; ... ultimately one must have one's experiences in common."

Fishing for Contacts

Networking events come in many forms and faces. The traditional event would be a societal open-day gathering or similar event; or perhaps a recreational club or other social meeting; or a more high-profile event such as a concert or to listen to a celebrity speaker. Whichever it is, there are certain things to bear in mind that will help your chances of success.

Similarly, you need to update yourself with appropriate information which the people you may meet find interesting – in other words, *the bait.*

Imagine you are going fishing. First you identify where your fish lives or what type of fishing it will be: salt water or fresh water. Then think about the type of place you could go to hook the type of fish you'd like to catch. By this I mean that the person who wishes to network to build up his or her potential client base needs to consider where they are likely to meet their prospects. It is relatively pointless to go to events where the chances of meeting a prospective client are non-existent. In other words, you need to go to a river or a part of the sea which has fish in it, not the part that's been over-fished to extinction. Then you need to decide if the tackle you have is suitable for the task. There is very little chance of success if you use a boat rod with a fly line, or use a coarse fishing rod for beach casting. Similarly, you need to update yourself with appropriate information which the people you may meet will find interesting - in other words, the bait.

It has been often said that each person you meet has the potential of helping you contact at least 10 more potential clients. Personally, I think the evidence for this is a little vague. Nevertheless, it certainly makes good sense to pitch to a bigger audience than a smaller one, unless exclusivity is part of the attraction for you, your service, or your product.

Unfortunately, many people at networking/social events still treat the occasion as if they are on a Japanese game show and rush around like headless chickens trying to collect as many name cards as possible. Happily, because of social media, and contact management Apps, cards are largely becoming redundant. Instead, people collect websites, social media details and WhatsApp addresses by typing them in at the time of hearing them. It's more efficient, less wasteful and effective. People talk about their Twitter feed, or their Instagram or Tik Tok posts. The news they have may come from Reddit or Facebook. In time, these will be replaced as newer platforms come online. Facebook is, at the time of writing, considered more for older people. However, it is evolving to become more of a marketplace.

But remember one thing: the person in front of you is more important. Talk to them, not your phone.

Sellers should always be subordinate to buyers.

I remember once meeting a Mr. H Chicken at an event a while ago who asked for my card. However, when I said that I had just run out and that the printers were making some new ones as we spoke –

actually the truth on this occasion – he looked ashen as if I had just committed the worst possible sin in networking. Then he assumed I was lying, joking or some combination of both, and insisted that I must have one somewhere. It was turning into a ridiculous farce where the card had taken on a greater importance than the person in front of him. As soon as he realised that he was not going to be successful, he indignantly closed the conversation and looked around the room for other trophies to collect. He also lost a potential sale as I was interested in sourcing insurance cover for a friend. Like most CEOs, COOs, CFOs and other captains of industry, the last thing they want is some ingratiating urchin pestering and haranguing their Personal Assistant trying to sell him or her their services. What they may be interested in is someone they feel they can trust and when the time comes that they want to consider insurance or whatever, they will remember you and search for your contact details. Sellers should always be subordinate to buyers.

On another occasion I was invited to a talk and networking event organised by the Unit Trust arm of a major bank. During the drinks and introductions, one rather naive bank representative joined our small group of mostly Asian middle-aged professionals. She was very eye-catching, and she used this to her advantage.

Her smile flashed a set of perfect, brilliant white teeth. Her long hair could have come straight from a shampoo advertisement, which she furtively tousled. And her sparkly eyes glistened with light moisture. However, it was clear that she thought she could use her charms to win her way into the hearts of everyone she met. Consequently, she was as stunned as an electrocuted mullet when one of the ladies in our group gave the very polite excuse that she didn't want to share her contact details. But when her girlish charms refused to work, and because everyone was watching, she became quite defensive and slightly arrogant at the same time. None of the people in my group invested in her bank's services.

I need to clear up one issue right away. People like attractive people. If you are lucky enough to be blessed with good looks - in whichever way they are culturally defined - then you have an advantage, but it is most definitely not the most important component. The crucial element is making the other person feel comfortable with themselves and you.

If and when you do exchange information with someone and you enjoy their company, you may decide to keep their details in an electronic App or file. And for sure, you're likely to put a face to the name the next day and probably the day or two after that. But then, unless you have exceptional re-call ability, you'll start to forget. So, after a while you'll start to wonder what you had in common, or why you enjoyed their company enough to keep their information. This is why I recommend writing something that's particular to that person as soon as you have a free moment. In fact, I recommend noting four things:

1. Where and when you met
2. Something that will help you recognise them again
3. Something you have in common
4. The best time to contact them again

By writing these items down, it will help jog your memory. You are then in a much better position and more confident if you (suddenly) meet them again. Oh, and one last thing if you still use business cards, please make sure it's environmentally friendly. It matters to more people than you might think. Consider using a contact management App instead.

Golden Guideline 3

When you meet people for the first time there is a great temptation to collect their contact details at the first opportunity: don't. Wait. Listen first. Collect after

Wait until you know a little bit more about the person or people you're talking to; get to know them to see if they really are people who could benefit from your details, and you from theirs. If they are, then collect their information or card and write a couple of things on the back to help you remember the person for when you meet again. If it's electronic, include one distinguishing point and add to it later.

Golden Guideline 4

Be selective.

It doesn't always have to be about business, you might find you actually enjoy the other person's company and share similar interests. You might even want to swap contact details to arrange a squash or futsal match or any other social event. And if you do use a business card, electronic or otherwise, then follow Seth Godin's advice: "I don't want to use a tool unless I'm going to use it really well. People don't want a mediocre interaction."

People are going to Look

On most occasions, particularly if your company has organised an event, you may be required to wear a name tag. This is all very well, but I need to clarify a few things here. There are some consultants who advise ladies to put their name tag on their right lapel. The reason for this is to stop people from looking across their breasts after shaking hands, if the name card is put on their left lapel. Well, here's the bottom line: if you are attractive to the other person, people are going to look irrespective of where you put your name tag. People look because of genetic conditioning or out of admiration, or to satisfy any latent curiosity, or out of desire or idle inquisitiveness. Whatever the reason, people will glance because the body is an incredibly important source of information to help a person dissect and understand the real message that someone puts across.

So of course they will glance at you, first at a subconscious level and then in various degrees with the conscious mind.

From a work perspective, there are still managers and bosses who think that if an employee is enjoying themselves, they are not really working.

Have fun and enjoy yourself – especially if the boss isn't there.

And this goes doubly so at networking events, which is a great shame as there's nothing more of a turn-off than having someone interact with you as if you've just entered a kitchen showroom and they want to sell you the latest tackiness from Korea. Have fun and enjoy yourself - especially if the boss isn't there.

Golden Guideline 5

If you go to a networking event as a group, make sure you mix with the clients, or at the very least, cater to their requests as best you can.

One other thing to remember. It may be tempting and 'safe' to talk with your colleagues, but you really are there to promote or, at a minimum, represent your company and its interests in the best way possible.

Stepping Outside the Comfort Zone

Many people I've met hate the idea of attending gatherings and avoid them as much as they can. And I can empathise completely. To go up to a complete stranger and introduce yourself takes a lot of courage and requires the person doing it to step outside their comfort zone. It can be a daunting task because lurking away in the dark depths of many people's minds is the semi-conditioned fear of rejection, and consequently the irrational risk of looking foolish. Think back to those teenage years when you started to find other people attractive. For many, that shyness never goes away. You are most certainly not alone.

It is a great shame in modern societies that so much importance is attached to rejection. It happens, and will happen in various formats throughout everyone's life, so the real issue is how to deal with it as best you can.

Emotions are one of the most, if not the most, infectious aspects of communication. Whatever you feel, the person you're talking with will, to varying degrees, also feel.

The answer, as with most of the challenging things in life, lies in mentally reframing the issue. The symptoms may be physical and real, but the issue is psychological. In other words, it's really all about how we perceive 'the problem'. The more concerned you are about what people think of you, the more the problem will rear its ugly head. So we need to deal with this.

Suffice to say at this point that we are moving away from this chapter's main focus and into a complex area which requires a more in-depth analysis. I cover this in detail in Chapter 7: EI & SI. It will also appear on occasions in other sections of this book since it is one of the central themes of communicating effectively. For this particular chapter, and to conclude this section, it is important to realise that emotions are one of the most, if not **the** most, infectious aspects of communication. Howsoever you feel, the person you're talking with will, to varying degrees feel the same – unless, that is, they live in the proverbial cave. So, if you are nervous about going up to strangers and introducing yourself, then the person you go up to is also likely to feel nervous about meeting you. Just being aware of this fact will help, but to completely overcome your fears requires a more careful reflection of who you are and what you really want from your work and life in general. The latter is a crucial question that you need to answer before you can really enjoy (and be enjoyed) at social and professional networking events.

> **'More business decisions occur over lunch and dinner than at any other time, yet no MBA courses are given on the subject.'**
>
> *Peter Drucker*

The Future of Social and Professional Networking

In the past it was all about a numbers game - and game is probably the best word for it - with the objective to meet as many 'prospects' as possible, and for them to become clients. The 'X' number is usually quoted as 10 new prospects. This we were reliably informed would lead to a deeper penetration of the business community and greater profit for the sales person. Profit underlined the rationale for all networking and this became the main reason for the growth in event organisers. Less so now. The sheer number of possibilities that the internet provides, is changing the way we do things. The transformation of the way we do business, particularly with mobile technology, has been life changing. And to think, not too long ago we had door-to-door salesmen. And no mobile phones. Electronic communication has now largely taken over for the buyer or seeker of services. And as soon as you click on something you're interested in, you will trigger myriad algorithms to connect you with more of the same or similar. In many ways, this will make the old style of networking events redundant. But not completely.

Networking still exists but it's changing. There are more online events, particularly in this time of Covid, and online platforms are growing in number and ease of use. There will also be more exclusivity as part of marketing strategy. Zoom events will become more accepted, even in rural areas in developing countries where internet access is less accessible. There is a large untapped market out there.

Currently it is possible to go to a market research company and identify households, even individuals, who are likely to be interested in your product and target them directly through social media advertising. That also holds true for products which they are not even aware that they want or need.

However, it has not all gone electronic yet. While there may be forums for just about everything, there are still physical get-togethers. Older, and generally wealthier, people often still prefer to feel the fabric and try on clothes before they buy them. Car test-drives haven't disappeared yet. They will, when augmented reality becomes more common, but not yet.

The future of networking is likely to become more and more electronic. This is great if you don't like meeting people face-to-face, but you will still need to present yourself effectively online. I will cover this in detail in Chapter 15. If you are middle-aged, my advice is to embrace the new technology since Gen Y and Z already have. It brings a mind-warping set of possibilities.

> **'The trick in life is to do things that are fun all the time.'**
>
> *Warren Buffett*

3. Personal Interactions: the dos and don'ts

> **Real answers need to be found in dialogue and interaction and, yes, our shared human condition. This means being open to one another instead of simply fighting to maintain a prescribed position.'**
>
> *Malcolm Boyd*

Engaging People

When you make conversation, there's very little worse than mentioning to a guy that his eyebrows have an incredible likeness to sea slugs, his breath has the pungent aroma of an Australian outback toilet, and his two waistlines give him the uncanny resemblance to a vertical wart hog. Similarly, you would not approach an attractive female and suggest that she has nice breasts, you think that her panty line compliments her behind, and that the real reason she's talking to you is because she wants to sleep with you. No!

However, there is another scenario which is up there with the previous two and that is to say nothing at all. Yet I see it all the time, and have also been on the receiving end more than once. It's the situation where two (usually two) people meet, exchange names and handshakes and then stare at each other with absolutely nothing to say except a formulaic 'How are you?' and the subconscious of both people are screaming at their respective conscious minds saying 'You idiot. Look what you've got us into this time.'

If you're meeting someone in an office, the main onus of responsibility on generating the small talk is on the person whose office it is. Conversely, if you are both in a neutral environment and you go up to someone, then it's more your responsibility than theirs. However, it's important to recognise that both parties enter into a verbal dance that requires active contributions from both participants. In other words, you need to be well-versed in the art of small talk.

Small Talk

It is an art that requires thought; it demands a small measure of intelligence, a spoonful of curiosity, a pinch of courage, and a slice of desire to find something in common with the other person.

There is an excellent quote by Zig Ziglar who states that "People don't care how much you know, until they know how much you care... about them." Unfortunately, modern cultures appear to be evolving with ever evolving technology which makes people less relevant. And this, I believe, is having an effect on the value people place on personal interactions. As a result of this, we seem to be heading towards an increasingly self-centred world. Yes, I agree that there are many exceptions, but as a general trend, I still maintain that we are moving in this direction.

Consequently, this has had quite an effect on the way we interact with each other. For example, have you noticed that people have less time than before to spend with you? Do they immediately look at their phone when a message comes in even though you are mid-sentence? Technically we all have the same amount of time, but these days we are expected to achieve more. However, small talk is an integral part of this interaction; it's just that it has to be done faster and more succinctly than before. Nevertheless, the quality must still be there.

So, what should you do?

The standard approach is to make a comment or question about the weather, the environment you're in, or something from the local or national news. And these are fine, with the caveat that you should have a genuine interest in the comment or question you make.

However, some advice is potentially disastrous such as complimenting the person on their appearance or clothing but not really meaning it. There is a very high chance that they will sense you are asking for the sake of making small talk and will therefore lower their estimation of you. And woe betide you if you lie i.e., you say their watch or jewellery is nice, but it's really not your cup of tea, or you really think it belongs in a kindergarten student's art class. Other subjects to avoid can include asking their opinion on something you have rigid views about. Or stating you hate something. In fact, it's best to avoid anything controversial, especially the first time you meet someone. Be positive.

These days people are more cognitively aware; not everyone, sure, but the population at large is generally becoming more knowledgeable regarding the mechanics of communication.

For that reason, I believe there is another and possibly better approach to personal interactions which adds a new dimension and may help with those awkward moments. The concept is really quite simple and comes as a two-part package:

1. **Be aware of your surroundings.**

This has two sub-parts: the place where the interaction occurs; and the wider environment. The former is about something immediate and shared. The latter is about more general subjects like the weather, news and locality etc.

2. **Be genuine.**

This also has two sub-parts: avoid negative messages such as "Looks like New Zealand are not going to make it any further in the World Cup, eh?" It would be much better to use a more positive question, such as "Who do you fancy in the next round?" The second sub-part is to avoid anything that invades the other person's core choices such as clothing, jewellery, personal photos, unless the compliment is genuine. For sure, if you like the same things then the 'getting to know you' stage will be quicker. And faster still if you share similar body language mannerisms, voice tone and pace, and conceptualise ideas in a comparable way.

Say something insincere and be prepared to dig yourself a hole to bury the miserable attempt at conversation in.

So, just to summarise the last paragraph: say something positive that you have a genuine interest in and you'll be on the right track. Say something insincere and then be prepared to dig yourself a hole to bury the miserable attempt at conversation in. In the extreme case that there is nothing about the other person that stimulates your mind, then either get down to business as soon as possible and stick to facts, or make a polite excuse to disappear.

While we're on the subject of avoiding idiocy and the need to wear a paper bag over your head in public or an extra-large facemask is the misconception that you have to discover the person's name at the earliest opportunity and use it as often as possible – think dated call-centre scripts. However, this can be almost as annoying as someone in an elevator squeezing out a silent one with the rampant odour of a gushing, sulphurous hot spring. Sorry for the analogy, but in all seriousness, incessantly repeating the other person's name thinking it makes the person you're talking to friendlier or more likely to enjoy your company then you really ought to get rid of that 'mullet' haircut, stop listening to 70s disco (except at retro-parties), and recognise that studying Tai Chi is not going to stop the ageing process. Finding out the person's name and using once or twice is fine, but the reason should be so that it ventures from short-term recall into short-term memory, and then into long-term memory. This can easily be achieved through mentally resaying the name in your head.

Putting people at ease

Let's face it, meeting people for the first time can be a bit scary, but then there is a high chance that they are thinking the same thing as you. And, after the initial handshake and greeting, people can become even more nervous about finding the right topic to talk about. So, putting people at ease is one of the most difficult parts of any interaction. But there is a way.

In addition to following points 1 and 2 above, you should make sure that you already have a 'wh' (what, where, when, who, which) or a 'how' question already in mind before you go up and greet them. As soon as you see people in the room, meeting, at an event, etc., you should be thinking of things to ask, rather than arrive, go straight to the bar or food table, or just stand there like fish out of water. By already having mentally prepared a couple of questions, you will also have a slightly more focussed look about you which will help ease the initial interaction. The use of 'wh' and 'how' questions ('open questions') have the advantage that the person you ask will usually have to give more than just a 'yes' or 'no' answer. In other words, they will give you information which will help you formulate the next statement or question. Then, before you know it, there will be a more relaxed atmosphere between the two of you, and the conversation will flow smoother as you position yourselves to topics you both enjoy discussing.

For the best situation, there needs to be a balance between sensitivity and self-confidence. On one hand we need to be confident, decisive and purposeful, yet on the other we need to make sure that we are not seen as overbearing, impatient and pushy. The latter will make it appear that our mission is to dominate the interaction. We need to make sure we are considerate, cooperative and responsive, yet we must also be aware if we are becoming timid, unquestioning and shy, as these qualities can also be just as detrimental to conversation.

Further, extreme sensitivity can lead to fear. Therefore, the optimum approach for putting people at ease is to balance self-confidence with sensitivity to get to a level of sociability. See Figure 1. The Interaction Matrix

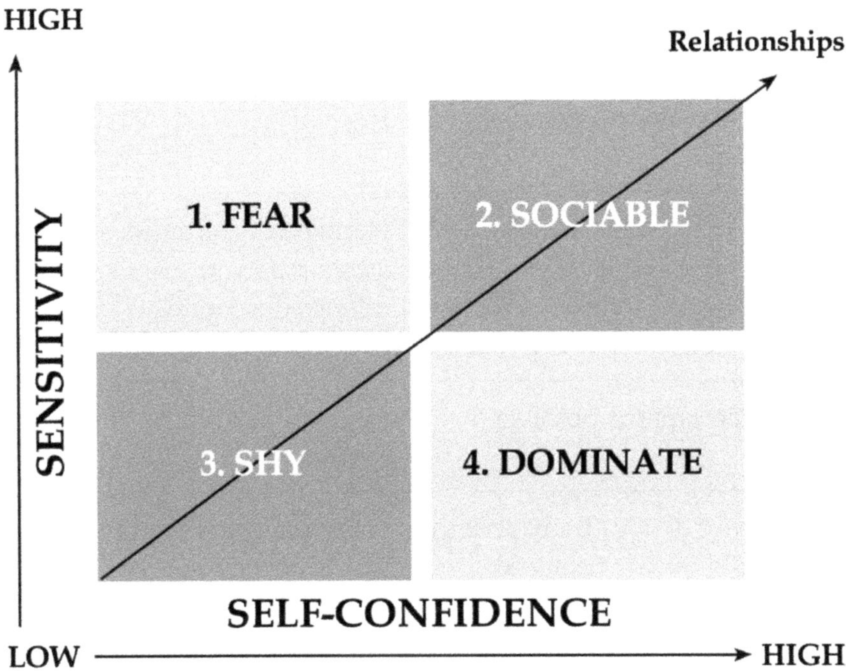

Figure 1: The Interaction Matrix

Golden Guideline

Asking a question to the other person(s) is great, but be very aware not to interrogate them. Create enough space for them to think and form a question of their own. And if the pause is starting to become too long, then you can help them out by para-phrasing your question.

The Dos and Don'ts

DO	DON'T
Be as positive as possible	Whinge or complain
Reflect on what went well and what didn't (and why)	Dwell in the past
Meet as many people as possible	Rush
Hand over your business details if asked, or if you think you may like to contact them in the future.	Hand out your business details as soon as you meet someone: it looks desperate.
Be as genuine as possible	Find faults with the other person
Be aware of your body posture - weight evenly balanced	Fold your arms or put your hands in your pocket
Give a short, firm handshake	Shake with a wet hand
Get to know the person	Try to 'sell' to every contact

Also have a look at the Dos and Don'ts in the Body Language section (see Chapter 8) as all of them can be applied here too. With this in mind it's worth pointing out that to be really excellent at engaging people, you should also be proficient at all the other skills discussed in this book. To isolate each area of communication - as this book does - is done solely for ease of organisation and structure. Doing it in topics and sections should help you, the reader, create mental images of the information and therefore make it easier for you to digest and use the knowledge. Nevertheless, it is worth reiterating that communication is more than just the sum total of individual parts. IT is about developing a greater awareness of the information from the subconscious to the conscious mind, and the ability to seamlessly integrate learned skills to effect a more efficient interaction.

'The dilemmas of interaction: how to decide on the facade we present to the world despite what's going on inside us.'

James Hancock

Summary

The reality of meeting and engaging people is that we do it every day: we constantly meet new people. And while these new people may be interested in either our friendship, service or product (or at least know of people who are), you would be well advised to consider them as acquaintances first (and friends later) before you even consider 'marketing' yourself or what you have to offer. And above all, remember to be as genuine as possible with people because they are becoming wiser to sales tricks and techniques, and will instantly shut you out if you use them. And besides, friendship has become underrated these days, so enjoy the person.

4. The Most Important Skill: listening

'Sometimes one creates a dynamic impression by saying something, and sometimes one creates as significant an impression by remaining silent.'

Dalai Lama

I still find it absolutely extraordinary that so many people I meet in Asia insist that one of their best skills is the ability to listen well. And, in a delicious twist of irony, as I ask them why they believe this, I notice through their body language, eye movement and verbal clues that they are immediately thinking about their reply even before all the information is presented. Yet their reply is filled with spurious justification as to why they are excellent at listening. Unfortunately, it is a fact that most people are very bad at listening, and there are some clear indicators of this I'd like to share with you. Are you guilty?

The 'Yes, but...' challenge

Perhaps the most identifiable pointer that people are not listening to you is that they begin their sentences with 'Yes, but...' What this is really saying is that they are focussing more on what they intend to say next rather than listening to you. It is, however, perfectly acceptable to begin a sentence with "Yes something, something, something, but..." which would suggest that they are repeating or reframing a piece of your information to ensure they understood you right before they contradict or offer an alternative. It's when the two words 'Yes, but...' come together that lets you know they are not really listening to you. Less obvious, but still an indicator of a person may not be paying full attention to you is beginning a sentence with the word 'But' on its own i.e., without the 'Yes' attached to it.

'Yes, but…' at the beginning of any sentence is very destructive: it's the same as saying "I'm not really listening to you because my thoughts and ideas are more important than yours." And what happens is that the subconscious of the other person picks up on little nuances like this and translates and relays them to the conscious mind in the form of frustration or even anger.

Actually, if you listen closely to other people's conversations, it soon becomes apparent how little people really listen to each other. You will quickly notice that the communication used in these interactions is quite ineffective for the purpose of understanding; there is little meaningful collaboration taking place. It's almost as if one army advances to attack while the other holds their ground. Then, at some undefined moment, the sides change and the other side attacks while the first tries to hold their ground. And all of this is due largely because of two little words 'Yes, but…'

Getting rid of the bad habit

Many people are unaware of how many times they begin sentences with 'Yes, but', or 'But....', so the first step to getting rid of this habit is to notice it. Therefore, sensitise yourself to the words and see the number of times you say them at the beginning of your sentences. At first it may seem that you don't say many at all, although this will probably be because you're missing most of them. As your detection of the problem grows, you'll be able to catch yourself saying more of them. Once you do that, you'll be in a better position to stop the words before you actually say them which will allow you to use alternative words and phrases instead.

Furthermore, it's a great way to see how much you really listen to other people. Quite simply, the more you develop your focussed listening skills, the better position you'll be in to counter or support other people's views, or offer an alternative solution if there's a problem to solve. And these solutions are more likely to be accepted because the subconscious of the person you're talking with will recognise that you're actively taking an interest in them and their ideas.

What you can say instead

There are many possibilities here, but one of the best is to try and use the word 'Yes' at the beginning, not necessarily that you agree with them, but to say you've understood what the other person's saying e.g., "Yes, I see what you mean, but..."

There is nearly always a way around using 'Yes, but...' and 'But…', and probably the best manner is to rephrase the message more positively. For example:

Avoid
"Yes, but I don't think that's the best solution to the problem."

Could be re-phrased
"I think there's a better way to solve the problem."

In fact, being more positive with your communication warrants a separate mention because it's an incredibly important element in the art of persuasion (See Chapters 9 and 11).

Sometimes you can just leave 'Yes, but…' it out altogether. For example:

Avoid
"Yes, but isn't that going to reduce profitability?"

Could be re-phrased
"Isn't that going to reduce profitability?"

Another way of disagreeing with the other person directly is to use the phrase '**Yes, and**'. For example, if you are accused of saying or doing something, which you didn't; or there's a misinterpretation of something you've said, and you need to restate what you really mean, you can use 'Yes, and…' For example:

Instead of
"Yes, but it wasn't my fault."

Rephrase the utterance to
"Yes, and I think I know where the problem lies."

Instead of
"Yes, but what I meant was..."

Say
"Yes, and what I mean by that is..."

Instead of
"Yes, but that's easier said than done."

State
"Yes, and also easier said than done."

If words are chosen well, the messages you say are more likely to be listened to with a greater chance of acceptance. Words are therefore the vehicle to carry the message, and the choice of appropriate vehicle is based on the situation. It would be unwise to take a patient to the hospital on a tractor. It could be done, but the ride would likely be very uncomfortable, and with the risk of further injury to the patient. Similarly, if you were chauffeuring a VIP it would be wise to use a limousine rather than a family hatchback. It could be done, of course, but then it would likely leave a very negative impression on the person travelling. In the same way, transporting everyday people by such an expensive and luxurious car may leave them suspicious and overly wary of the other person's intentions. Therefore, communication is best when the right vehicle is used for the right people. In other words, the right words.

If words are chosen well, the messages you say are more likely to be listened to with a greater chance of acceptance.

The Loathsome Advisor

Non-Alpha people tend to make better listeners as they avoid jumping to the first idea they have, and wait until they've heard the full scope of the concern.

This type of listener is unfortunately very common and is particularly the case with Alpha-type personalities. Alpha-type people tend to want to solve problems. I find this interesting because I notice that they are often not so good at solving their own problems as they are at resolving other people's issues. Non-Alpha-type personalities, on the other hand, and I know I run the risk of criticism with these huge generalisations, tend to make better listeners since they avoid hanging on to the first idea which jumps into their head and wait until they have heard the full scope of the concern.

Of course, there are some excellent Alpha-type listeners too. However, on the whole it seems that they listen only long enough until they think they understand the matter and have their own version of how to immediately solve it. The risk here is that they interrupt with their solution before the speaker may have had the time necessary to explain all the little nuances of the issue. Yet for the *Advisor*, the job is done and the subject over with, unless the Advisor is prompted to now speak on *their* experiences of *their* problem. In other words, they are bad listeners.

You can usually identify the *Advisor* since he or she often uses phrases such as 'What you need to do...'; 'Why don't you...'; 'All you need to do is...' and so on. Another key problem the *Advisor* has – and a good way to identify these people – is that they often begin their sentences with the phrase 'Yes, but...' As mentioned above, this is a pretty clear indication that the listener is thinking more about his or her reply than to what you are really saying. And unfortunately, the subconscious of the speaker's mind picks up on little nuances like this, which is why the *Advisor* can be such a loathsome person as a conversation companion.

Regrettably, people are only half aware that they are doing this because our socially-conditioned, in-built setting is to focus more on the message we want to say rather than on the way we say it. The good news is that things are changing and people are now becoming much more aware of the need to present a message in a way to cater more to the listener's ear rather than simply rely on our default way of speaking.

Are you guilty?

If you are reading this in the morning, then for the rest of the day count the number of times the people you talk with use the words 'Yes, but...' or 'But...' at the beginning of sentences. Once you condition yourself to recognising this, you'll be in a better position to recognise it when *you* say the

phrases yourself. Then, to make your communication as effective as possible, train yourself to say 'Yes, and...' or something other than 'Yes, but...'

That's the first indicator that the person you are speaking with is not really listening – the *Loathsome Advisor,* but there are three main others.

The Selfish Shifter

This type of person scrutinizes then probes what the speaker is saying, but rather than to encourage them, the reason they ask questions is to shift the conversation away from the speaker's choice. This type of listener prefers the sound of their own voice rather than anybody else's, and they quickly shift the topic to one they would rather talk about.

Certainly, in any conversation there is a two-way dialogue. Even when one of the participants is predominantly listening, there is still the interaction of questions and answers. The difference is that the *Shifter* is asking to steer the topic, while the good listener asks questions to encourage the speaker to elaborate more on what they wish to speak about. For sure, we are all a little guilty of this when we start to get bored with the subject, but at least we usually wait until we feel that the speaker has had ample time to express themselves. The *Selfish Shifter* doesn't wait for this and is quite happy to interrupt the speaker whenever they feel they can get away with it, without seeming overly rude. For example, the speaker may be talking on the subject of buying clothes in their local night-market; a good listener would then ask a question about their recent purchases, or perhaps how often they go, or something that they feel would aid the speaker to continue with their story. The poor listener – the *Selfish Shifter* – would be more likely to ask whether they had visited a night market in the listener's area, or if they had heard about what the listener had bought recently.

The difference between the two types of questions is subtle, but quite profound in their effects. At the early stages of a conversation, it may be difficult to detect this type of poor listener, because the speaker is being asked a question which, at a certain neuro-semantic level, feels good. However, with the selfish questions, the speaker will, after a while, start to feel as though they are not really being listened to, or frustrated that the topic shifts away from what they were talking about. And if they try to return to their original topic, they find that it's either ignored or again steered away.

Are you guilty?

The next time you're in a conversation, note the questions that come to mind as the speaker continues. But just before you ask them, take a nano-second or two to ask yourself if they're designed to extract more information (and therefore encourage the speaker), or are they to steer the topic to something more interesting for you. And, if you find that this is too difficult to do, then there is a good chance that the reason is you don't care enough about what the other person is saying in the first place.

The Insidious Interpreter

This particular listener drives most people up the wall. I also notice that it's used a lot by people who think that they have some sort of authority, or see themselves as superior to they're speaking with - this could be through age, experience, title, rank, etc. The key thing about this type of conversation partner is that they twist almost everything you say to what *they think* you would like to say. For example, if you say that you plan on going to the coast for the weekend, they may state back to you something like "I expect you're tired of the countryside these days." or "Yes, you've been working very hard recently, haven't you?" These are purposefully interpreting questions.

Although they seem fairly innocuous at first, they are clear indications that the other person is interpreting what you're saying rather than listening for your real meaning. They can't be bothered with you and just interpret *they* think you mean. In other words, they are poor listeners. Another example was when I was in conversation with a 'sweet, elderly lady' – actually not so sweet, and as mad as a hatter, but that's another story. I mentioned that I would be travelling a lot over the next few weeks. I was then subjected to a barrage of statements that acted as questions such as: "Your business is doing well this year, then?"; "You have a lot of frequent flyer points to use, I suppose?"; and "You'll be visiting your family, of course?"

This type of listener is actually quite easy to spot as he or she will ask you questions which are phrased as statements. And this can quickly become so irritating that you'd rather have a conversation with a plank of wood. It's a shame that little old ladies don't come with a warning label to say whether they are bad listeners or not.

Are you guilty?

Simply listen to whether your questions are really phrased as questions with words such as 'what, where, who, when, which, why, how', or whether they are statements with a rising intonation at the end to force them into questions. In other words, are you trying to explain another person's motives and behaviour based on your own experiences and therefore trying to figure the other person out? If so, you may be guilty of interpreting. I suppose we all do this on occasion, but the key point is whether it becomes an annoying habit i.e., we use statements as questions all the time, or whether they just slip out infrequently.

The Evil Evaluator

This type of listener is merely listening to see if they agree or disagree with what you're saying: they're judging you. You see, if all they're doing is listening to you to evaluate if you are in concord with them, then the focus of attention of the listener is on them, not on the speaker. If the *Evaluator* agrees with what the speaker is saying, then they may encourage the speaker to say more. However, if the *Evaluator* disagrees with what the speaker is saying from the outset, then they will have little interest in encouraging the speaker say more. It's far more likely that the listener will override them with their objections.

One of the greatest problems with giving a presentation is the level of confidence of the speaker. And the lack of confidence is primarily due to the feeling of being judged. If a person feels judged then they generally tend to perform poorer than they would otherwise. This is the same principle as to why people in conversation feel less comfortable talking to certain people more than others. No-one likes to feel judged: it's a debilitating feeling. Unfortunately, the person judging – the *Evaluator* – will assume that the speaker isn't aware of what they are thinking, but this is incorrect. A lot of communication takes place at a subconscious and non-verbal level. While the speaker may not be tacitly aware that what they say is being evaluated, they will be aware that something is not as it should be. This feeling could manifest itself in irritation, frustration, a desire to finish the topic and talk about something else, or just to talk to someone else.

This type of bad listener is the most common because we all evaluate to a certain extent. We judge what others say based on our own understanding of the topic, and if we feel that we have the greater knowledge, we may choose to interrupt or stay quiet.

It could be argued that we naturally have an opinion and therefore agree or disagree with the speaker's opinions. We decide if something is morally right or wrong based on our socio-cultural upbringing. It's almost as if it's inbuilt to our system of understanding. However, we should also be aware that it is also potentially harmful to the interaction.

Are you guilty?

The next time you are in a conversation, particularly when the other side is relating a story or event, see if you encourage the conversation by uttering phrases such as "Yes, I think so too"; "Did he/she/it/they really…?"; "You're right/wrong"; "Surely not" and so on. The idea is to see how you react to things you agree or disagree with and how you verbalise it. Of course, it's only natural to have opinions on things: it proves you have an intellect. However, it's the degree that the opinions interfere with the other person's dialogue. If you really want to fully understand what the other person has to say/offer, then you have to listen with an open mind rather than just agreeing or disagreeing.

BECOMING A BETTER LISTENER

To be a good listener, people need to ***feel*** as though they are being listened to. And this is something you can't fake. The more sensitive the person is, the greater the likelihood that they will know if you are being genuine with them or not. Conversely, if they are the equivalent of a D flat on the evolutionary scale, then they may be happily oblivious to any wrong doings. But then ask yourself, are you really likely to find yourself engaged in such conversations anyway? Probably not.

Steven Covey wrote the excellent truism "To communicate effectively with me, you must first understand me." This is precisely what people want when they communicate with others: they want to be understood. However, there's more to it than this. People also want to feel empowered, and good listening is the key to this. Regrettably it seems that there are more bad listeners than good, and although this will often vary depending on whom you are listening to and the topic of conversation, it's probably fair to say that we could all benefit from improving our listening skills.

The first thing to do is to be aware of what you say and then think about how it sounds from the listener's perspective. This is an incredibly important skill to master, but a very challenging one since it's a lot of information to process at one time. You not only have to focus on what the other person is saying, but you also have to listen to your own words and process how they might be interpreted by the other side.

The second method to improve your listening skill is to focus on trying to understand how the speaker feels when they are speaking. This is called empathic listening and it gives the listener huge clues as to why the person is saying what they are saying. It helps the listener understand the emotions involved for the speaker, which could go a long way to explain their choice of words and intonation.

The third improvement vehicle builds on the second by getting the listener to monitor whether they are wishing to interrupt or reply before the speaker has finished what they were saying. Is the focus of the listening to reply or is it to fully explore what the speaker has to say? It should be the latter. So, bite back the craving to interrupt and instead consider more what the speaker is trying to articulate. Don't worry about forgetting what you were planning to say: if it was important, you'll remember again. And if you do forget, then it is most likely that it was a reaction rather than a positive addition to the topic.

Dos and Don'ts

DO	DON'T
Mentally summarise	Show impatience
Listen for commonality	Stop listening
Concentrate on the speaker	Get easily distracted
Pause before answering	Interrupt
Ask questions	Shift subject if bored
Encourage the speaker	Interpret
Be aware of body language	Advise
Be aware of emotions	Evaluate

I know that you believe you understand what you think I said, but I'm not sure you realise that what you heard is not what I meant.'

Robert McCloskey

Summary

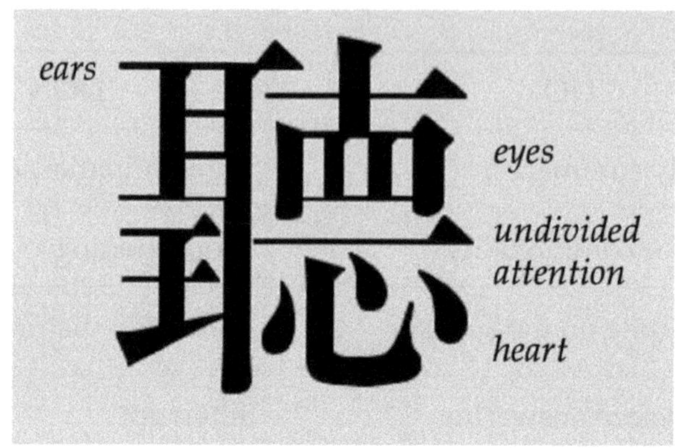

This older, more complex Chinese character for listening has several sub-characters within it: ears, eyes, heart, undivided attention, and scholar (underneath 'ear'). And these sub-characters form important clues as to how we should listen. We should use our ears for the sounds; our eyes to get visual feedback from the body language and facial expressions that the person uses; we should use our heart to understand the feelings the speaker has with the words; and we should give our undivided attention to the speaker. This is how the wise listen. Finally, we should also listen for what is expected but avoided because, as Peter Drucker points out, "The most important thing in communication is to hear what isn't being said."

5. Questioning Skills

'Answers are easy to find. It's asking the right question that's difficult.'

David Hirst

Picture this: you need some information from someone else - it could be about a process, a confirmation, a set of instructions, a formula, etc. So, you ask the relevant question to get, you hope, the answer you need. Then why are there so many mistakes, so many jobs done incorrectly, so many misunderstandings? Part of the answer lies in the fact that people question other people badly. The other part of the equation is the listener, because we know people generally think they listen better than they actually do. Some studies have found that people only listen to around 20% of what's being said to them in a conversation. And I've found from personal experience that people will only hear what their brain is tuned to. An example of this is when I was in the outskirts of Tokyo and asked in passable Japanese which bus goes to Shinjuku – I'd already passed my first Japanese language exam, and my speaking was adequate, but my knowledge of Kanji (Chinese characters) was very limited, hence the question. The lady replied in Japanese that she was sorry, but she couldn't speak English and therefore could not tell me which bus to take. I mentioned (in Japanese) that I could understand her perfectly and all she needed to do was point me in the right direction of the appropriate bus. She then apologised again and said that her English just wasn't good enough. She was convinced that whatever I was saying was in English because she hadn't considered the possibility that I was speaking in Japanese or even another language for that matter. However, the next person I asked managed to point out the correct bus therefore validating my linguistic ability. Consequently, it's true that people often hear only what they want to hear. Nevertheless, to reduce the possibility of miscommunication as much as possible, we also have to look at the questioner: it takes two to tango, or in this case communicate.

Let's make a big assumption that the listener will willingly give you answers. In this case, there are certain questions you really should try to avoid if you want to get the best answer.

'Judge a man by his questions rather than by his answers.'

Voltaire

Leading Questions

These are questions that suggest or 'lead' the listener to an answer that may or may not be true. For example: "You're interested in this section, aren't you?" or "Don't you think the weather's strange for this time of year?" In both cases the questioner makes it more difficult for the answerer to contradict them. To answer either of the above questions in the negative or 'No' would be to take an antagonist stance. It is why many people are quite happy to go along with whatever the premise is initially, even if they disagree with it.

Sales people will often use these leading questions to get their 'target' in a 'Yes' frame of mind before they spring whatever trap it is they are tracking towards.

"I assume you want the best deal from your investments, don't you?"

"But I also see that you would like to minimise the risk factors with whichever investments you decide on, wouldn't you?"

"Because this particular unit trust has outperformed many of the others, it has quite a lot going for it, doesn't it?"

For sure, the situation and intonation used will have a large effect on the interaction, but I'm sure you get the gist of what I'm trying to put across, can't you.

Multiple Questions

For example, "Would you prefer staggered time off, a smaller monetary allowance, larger insurance coverage, or would you like to think about it for a while?" The likely answer is that the person would like to think about it, because the golden rule with multiple questions is that the respondent is probably only going to answer the last question, not the others. Another example would be "Were you annoyed, upset, or it didn't bother you?" Again, the person answering is likely to reply 'Yes' or 'No', but unless the person expounds on the answer, the questioner will be unaware of which of the feelings the other person really felt. Further, the longer the question, the more likely the respondent is to just answer the last part of the question. This is because it requires a greater cognitive capacity to manage all the variables as they appear – this is also known as the 'Recency Effect'.

Certainly, in most cases 'either or' questions prove very little trouble for most people and can be used to save time. Problems only really start when the variables increase to a point where the intended answerer is confused, then they are likely to give up and just answer the last part of the question.

Hypothetical Questions

Try answering this question: What would you have read if you hadn't decided to read this? Yes, it's a bit of a strange question, because you *are* reading this and not anything else. What I'm trying to exemplify here is that it is strange to ask about something you are not reading at the specific time of not reading it. Confused? Well, I'm not surprised because it's an example of a hypothetical question.

The main problem with this type of question is that because they are hypothetical in nature, they can only produce hypothetical answers, which may or may not become fact. A very common example of the problem is the use of the second conditional in English. For example: What would you do if you won the jackpot or the lottery? The question invites the respondent to theorise on their possible actions, which may bear little relationship to what they would do if they really did win. Therefore, if you ask a hypothetical question, be prepared for a hypothetical answer.

However, they can be extremely useful - some would say essential - in negotiations as they invite possibilities and test people's positions on sensitive subject areas without getting into any confrontation. We will revisit hypothetical questions, particularly 'If' questions, in the chapter on negotiating.

So, what are the best questions to get information?

Unfortunately, the somewhat enigmatic answer to this fairly straightforward question depends on what type of information you're trying to get. I've therefore divided questions into three main types:

1. **LOGICAL (OPEN) Questions**
2. **YES / NO Questions**
3. **CREATIVE Questions**

Without doubt, an applied linguist could further (and more accurately) sub-divide these into other groups. But for the purposes of communicating with anyone, we'll stick to three.

1. *Logical (Open) Questions*

> **'I keep six honest serving-men (They taught me all I knew): Their names are What and Why and When, and How and Where and Who.'**
>
> ***Rudyard Kipling***

This category is also known as the 'Journalist's Six', as they are the absolute basics for finding answers to tell a story effectively. They are also known as 'Open Questions' because the answer to them is open i.e., you don't know exactly what the answer will be. For example:

1. Who's involved? Who will it affect? Who will benefit? Who may object? Who will do it?
2. What went wrong? What should happen next? What led to the success? What could be done?
3. When will it take place? When are the various stages? When did it occur?
4. Where should it take place? Where else is possible? Where else is affected?
5. Why the location? Why the time? Why the people? Why this and not that? Why not?
6. How does this affect…? How can it be improved? How can it be described? How can it be dealt with?

These are excellent questions for finding out information. They get the respondent to talk about the subject in more detail. In some cases, the question can simply be re-phrased by selecting a different question word, but the principle of logic remains the same. Let's now compare these with Yes/No questions.

2. *Yes/No (closed) Questions*

These are also great questions if used well as they confirm or deny propositions. Unfortunately, because they elicit a simple answer, they are used when 'open' questions would be better, leading to one of the most common types of miscommunication: assumption.

Closed questions are those which can be answered with either 'Yes' or 'No'. For example: Are you enjoying this chapter? The answer is one of two responses – I'm taking answers such as 'Sort of' to be negative. The problem with this type of question is that it doesn't give you much information. For example, I don't know why you are or aren't enjoying it, or what causes the answer. Because of this, questioners should always begin with open questions before confirming – they nearly always go hand-in-hand.

Asking an open question to garner information and then make a decision based on that alone is riskier without adding a Yes/No question to confirm your assumptions.

For example, if I ask the open question, "What would you like to do tonight?" and you reply "It would be nice to eat out later." It would be reasonable to extrapolate that you'd like to go to a restaurant for dinner, and therefore you could argue that there's no need for a Yes/No question.

However, if we add a closed question, we can confirm whether this assumption is correct or not. For example, "Is it to be a restaurant night then?" The answer will then confirm your assumption. Similarly, you could also ask another open question with the assumption attached, "Which restaurant would you like to go to?" The respondent would then have to answer with the name of the restaurant (or type of food), or suggest something different such as "I was thinking more along the lines of a BBQ in the garden." It could also be argued that asking a confirming question when the assumption is very probable defeats the purpose of effective questioning, and I would agree. The real value of Yes/No questions is when you are trying to confirm complex information which might have different interpretations.

In summary of Open and Yes/No questions, I suggest that if open questions were used more in communication before leaping to Yes/No questions, there would be so many fewer mistakes.

However, Yes/No questions do have an important role to play after you have explored all the open question possibilities. They may not always be necessary with simple situations, but in the case of receiving or giving complex instructions, it's always a good idea to confirm.

3. *Creative Questions*

There is one fundamental when it comes to asking questions then it's this: if you ask the same question about the same situation, you'll get the same answer. It can be incredibly challenging just to be creative, particularly when you are under some sort of pressure to come up with a creative solution to a problem. Yet we are all asked to 'think outside the box'. It's all very well to say, but how do you do it? The answer is to re-frame the problem, or see it from alternative perspectives. For example, if you are stuck in a job that you can't stand, and every time you ask yourself the question "What do I really want to do?" you come up blank. And no matter how hard you try, you can't seem to come up with many ideas, then this is the time to use creative questioning. Try the following example.

> Now what car/vehicle you would like to own? ___________
>
> What are the characteristics of that vehicle that attracts you to it?
>
> 1.
> 2.
> 3.

One workshop participant who did this with me recently said she would like the new Volkswagen Beetle because of the following:

1. 'It looks neat and fashionable'
2. 'It's the right-size car for me – not too big, not too small'
3. 'It's reasonably economical'

The answers can be quite revealing because for many people a car is simply a means to get from A to B. They have very little interest in it other than when they have to pay the service bill or fill it with fuel. However, if we analyse the VW Beetle answers in more detail, we can interpret the following:

1. Looks are important. Out of all the possible answers, 'looks' came first. Now if we re-frame this to jobs, we can see that the title or job position may be important. It is how the job sounds or 'looks' to others which is important.

2. The person appears quite pragmatic and realistic with the next answer. Nothing ostentatious here. I would interpret this answer for work as looking for a position that's not too demanding but not boring either. They have no desire to quickly leap into management before they're ready.

3. The answer to the third question indicates that money is high-ish on the importance list, perhaps even more than job satisfaction. Therefore, this person needs to find a position where the salary

is slightly above average for the role.

I fully agree that these are my interpretations and they could be perceived completely differently by someone else. However, the main purpose of this exercise is to get people to see their problems from completely different perspectives. And by doing so, it's therefore possible to produce ideas that would have otherwise never have been considered.

The person then compared the description of her current job as a car with the description of the VW Beetle and saw the disparity i.e., what's missing in her job. The outcome? Well, actually this is a true story and she resigned from her current job and went to live in Australia where she is now very happily settled.

The job? Still in the tourism industry as far as I know, but the main point is that by asking creative questions, she was able to re-frame her life and put it in a new perspective.

If you are still unsure about what you would like to do (work-wise) in the future, you should first generate descriptions for your current job in terms of what it means to you. Then you should do an internet search for all the jobs that fit the key elements of those descriptions. This should create a whole host of new job ideas which may never have been considered if you were just asking the same question "What job do I want to do in the future?"

The beauty of this approach is that you can apply it to pretty much anything. For example, instead of using cars to come up with creative descriptions, you could think of food. How would you describe your current job as a dish of food? Would it be spicy, bland, tasty, aromatic…? And so on. Then compare the type of food you would like to eat if everything was available – bear in mind that you'd get bored if you had lobster every day, to say nothing of the cholesterol.

Creative questions can also be used to generate any number of different scenarios. For example, have a look at the following and see if they might change your standpoint on things.

1. What is it about your life that reminds you of what you liked/hated at school?
2. If you were made redundant tomorrow, what would you do to enhance your chances of getting another or better job?
3. What could you do with a small budget to contribute to your favourite charity?
4. What family member reminds you of your job, and why?
5. How would you change your communication with colleagues if everyone could hear what you said?

Think of something naturally different from your problem and then relate it to the issue using as many adjectives as possible.

The only real barrier to using creative questions is that it seems as though you need to be creative in the first place to use them effectively. However, this is false. All you need to remember is that you have to think of something naturally different from your problem e.g., a sport, a mode of transport, a book, a holiday destination, etc., and then relate it to the issue using as many adjectives as possible. It is the adjectives that reveal disparities and similarities. These then become the starting point for your search for a solution.

Using Empathy in Questions

The key aspect of empathic questions is that they reflect the feelings of the person whom you are communicating with. Although this term is usually associated with listening skills, it's equally relevant to questioning. It simply means that you phrase your question in a tone that expresses empathy for the person being asked. It is particularly useful in stressful or difficult situations such as job appraisals, interviews, enquiring about an event that went wrong, a personal sadness and the like. Using empathy is also an excellent way towards calming potentially aggressive situations. For example, in the case of a car accident, when tempers are on the edge of breaking, questions such as the following are quite likely.

"Why didn't you look where you were going?"
"Why didn't you use your indicators?"
"What were you thinking of with that manoeuvre?"

These and plenty more like them can be phrased either in an aggressive or an empathic way. More empathic phrasing would result in variations of the following:

"What distracted your attention?"
"Are your indicators working?"
"Why did you turn at that particular point?"

Keep in mind though, the phrasing is much less important than the way the questions are said i.e., the intonation. It's this – the manner of speech – that creates empathic value. You could also argue that in this sort of situation you are unlikely to want to show empathy, particularly if it's the other person's fault. Nevertheless, you are much more likely to arrive at a satisfactory solution and sooner than you would do otherwise.

Empathy in questions, listening and phrasing will also be looked at in relation to other aspects of communication in the chapters on 'Negotiations' and 'Emotional Intelligence'.

'Learn from yesterday, live for today, hope for tomorrow. The important thing is not to stop questioning.'

Albert Einstein

Summary

Failing to confirm assumptions is arguably one of the most common mistakes made in communication. And all it takes is a few simple questions to be sure that you have things right. But people would still rather risk making horrendous mistakes than ask what they feel their conversation partner will perceive as a 'dumb' question. It won't be, providing you phrase it in a way that clearly shows you understand their meaning, but want to make perfectly sure you have all the information and recognise the nuances the speaker wishes.

If you would like to improve your creative ability, or just be a little better at extracting information, then honing your questioning skills is a good place to start.

6. Giving and Receiving Advice, Compliments and Criticism.

'If one person says that you are a horse, smile at them.

If two people say that you are a horse, give it some thought.

If three people say you are a horse, go out and buy a saddle.'

Proverb

Giving and receiving advice is a little like going to the dentist: no one relishes it, but most of us realise that it's necessary and is likely to be beneficial in the long run. You would normally think that giving criticism is far easier than receiving it, but in fact most people I know dread the task.

And from the other person's perspective, whenever they hear or sense they are about to receive criticism for something, they immediately prepare for the worst. Whether they feel guilty about something, I'm not sure, but the person criticising is usually greeted with a guarded attitude from the people concerned. In fact, attitudes can range from not caring, to hope, to animosity, and everything in-between. So, although the person giving the comment knows the message they wish to put across, they first have to deal with whatever attitude they're faced with from the receiver. They then must ensure that the person is open to the information they're about to receive. This requires good communication skills, especially Emotional and Social Intelligence. This even applies to giving compliments which should, in theory, be much easier. However, I know of many people who are pretty bad at this too.

Giving Compliments

When was the last time you went up to a friend or colleague and gave them a compliment?

Imagine this: A friend of yours who you like to be with compliments you for doing something well. Or your boss comes up to you and 'out of the blue' pays you a compliment about your work. The chances are that you would feel really good for the rest of the day, be more productive, more positive and therefore probably easier and more enjoyable to work with. Now imagine your friend or boss scowling at you, or giving you one of those heavy sighs that says all is not well. How would you feel then? You see how something very simple can have a great effect on someone's emotions and reactions.

In a more formal context, particularly if you are the boss, the best way to deliver a compliment is to let the person know as soon as possible that the feedback they are about to receive is good news. This way, you immediately put the person at ease and the meeting can progress quickly. Unfortunately, some managers tease the individual and take a long time to get to the point which is nothing more than ego tripping and an unnecessary ordeal for the recipient.

In a less formal context it's easier, yet it is still something which some people have difficulty with. Yes, it has a lot to do with their upbringing and whether the environment they had as a child was less oppressive and more open. However, people can and do change.

From a work perspective, the only real issue with giving positive feedback is that there is a risk, albeit small, that the member of staff may feel that they are doing already great and they don't need to progress further. They don't feel the need to grow and change as the company grows and changes. They may take the meeting as vindication that everything's fine and they can rest on their laurels for the rest of their employment with that company. Consequently, even giving positive feedback takes a little more skill than simply saying 'well done' or giving some bonus or benefit. While any positive feedback should be vindication that the member of staff (or team) is on the right track with their work, its primary motive should be encouragement for the person or people to do more and to keep growing in the company.

Golden Guideline for Giving Positive Feedback at Work

Make sure the message has focus. Let them know what, where, when, and why, so the person can replicate what was good, minimise what needs to be improved, and have a course set to generate positive feedback in the future

Giving Constructive Criticism

This is where the going gets tough, and the weak hide in a small dark room. Most people today are starved of constructive feedback, especially from friends or the people who they think they can trust the most. However, giving this type of advice is really not as difficult as you might imagine it to be. The key is to focus on the effect of the positive change. For example, what will the change you need lead to, both for you and them with emphasis on the latter? The following is a suggested process that highlights this approach.

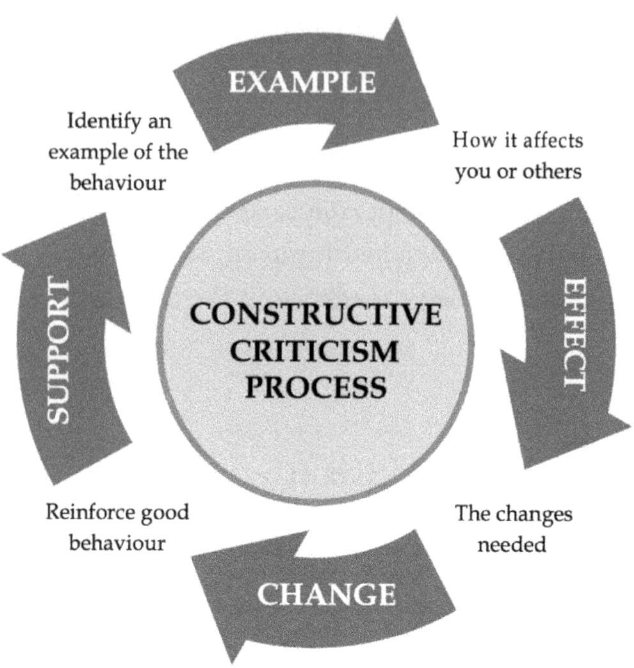

The Constructive Criticism Process

Starting at the top, you need to present an example of the behaviour that you've observed. This needs to be kept as factual as possible with no added emotions or opinions at this stage. For example: "I noticed that this is the third time this week that you've left the dishes in the sink when we agreed that I would do the dinner dishes if you did the breakfast ones."

This leads to examples of how this behaviour affects you or other people. Again, the evidence needs to be presented as factually and as measurable as possible – keep the emotions out. For example: "I had to spend time doing them before I left the house, which made me late for work."

The next part of the cycle is change. You need to show the person what change you believe is possible and how to go about it. It is crucial at this stage to ensure the person receiving the criticism has input to the change process as it will result in a much greater degree of commitment. For example: "How can we make sure they get done in the morning?"

The final part of the cycle is to reinforce the new behaviour with positive support and feedback. For example: "Thanks for doing the dishes this morning: I know we had a late night, last night, and you were in a hurry this morning too."

I see it as both a cyclical and linear model. It is a cyclical process because I believe change happens all the time, in fact we should always be on the lookout for new ways of doing things to keep life interesting. However, it can also be linear to correct a one-off, work situation problem.

Example: "These figures don't agree with the various project costs."
Effect: "I had to give up my weekend to get them ready for today."
Change: "What can we do to make sure this doesn't happen again?"
Support: "Your idea of asking someone to proof read is working well."

Golden Guideline for Giving Constructive Criticism

Example – what behaviour you have observed

↓

Effect – what result does this behaviour have on you or other people

↓

Change – let them know or ask them what behaviour you want from them

↓

Support – reinforce good behaviour

Sensitive Issues

Sensitive issues are situations where another person has a habit or behaviour that irritates the hell out of you. It could be that they chew their food with their mouth open, making a lot of noise in the process. Or they have a habit of cracking their knuckles every ten minutes. Or they wear noisy jewellery that clinks together and distracts you from your reading, watching TV or work. You can usually avoid the first example for most of the time, and if you find yourself in a situation where you're forced to sit with them, then you may be better off just putting up with it. But with the second two examples you may not be able to avoid the situation. And if it starts to affect your attitude or behaviour, then you need to do something about it.

Perhaps the biggest issue when giving this type of criticism is having the confidence to do it well and without malice. It's all very well saying to people 'be more confident', but the real issue is 'how?' How can you improve your confidence level? To answer this, we need to look at what makes human beings 'tick'. We have to look at the essence of confidence, and to do this we need to answer a few soul-searching questions about ourselves. For example, what do you like about yourself? If you can't find anything to like about yourself, how can you expect others to like you? Let's try another: what do you respect about yourself? Again, if you find it difficult to answer this question then it is absolutely certain that other people will have difficulty answering this question about you too. Further, it doesn't seem to get any easier as you climb the corporate ladder.

Being evaluated is what makes us feel uncomfortable and scrapes away at our self-confidence

The most common answers to the first question above are things such as integrity, honesty, happy-go-lucky, and so on. And these are great characteristics, but few people say anything about their physical selves? The reason for this is that people have a natural dislike for being judged or evaluated; people like to remain in their comfort zones. You see, if a person mentions something about their physical selves, it is instantly up for evaluation by everyone else within hearing distance. You can literally see it on their faces. So, when someone says something about their hair, eyes or feet, all the people around them turn to have a look and make their own comparisons and judgements. It's this evaluation that makes us feel uncomfortable and scrapes away at our self-confidence.

Therefore, we need to be able to create our own comfort zone when we deal with people in difficult situations such as giving criticism about sensitive issues.

When everything goes bad, you have yourself. Whenever you are tasked with difficult communication, you have to rely on yourself. Consequently, it is crucial that you identify the positive elements you like about yourself. Cast your mind back to college or university. Can you remember that some classmates were more popular than others? What made them more popular than the rest? You may think it was attractiveness, and to a certain extent that's probably true. Although, as they say, 'beauty is in the eye of the beholder'. Studies suggest that the main reason for their popularity was that they had an outgoing, gregarious and positive character. And this is all made possible by the fact that they were more comfortable with themselves (including all the bits they would have liked to change) than the rest of the people around them. Positive people attract other positive people and those whom would like to be more positive.

Negative people, and those with low self-esteem, attract like-minded people – there's more on this in chapter 9: The Law of Attraction.

There's one more part to understanding and developing confidence which is to recognise that fear is a natural phenomenon: it's all to do with the unknown.

Were you ever frightened of the dark as a small child? If yes, it was quite an irrational fear when you think about it. We were more frightened of what 'might' be in the dark – especially after watching a scary movie. Our imagination ran riot as to what 'might' be out there. And was it? Didn't we all wake up safe the next morning?

The unknown can generate a powerful, paralysing fear, and one we have to deal with before we can present a difficult message clearly. The bizarre thing is that most people, as we mentioned earlier, are actually starved of the constructive criticism they need to either enjoy a better social life, or to perform better at work and receive positive feedback in the future. The only real barrier to them receiving it ourselves.

When dealing with sensitive issues, the unknown is really how the person is likely to react to the criticism. Of course, the more times you give advice in this type of situation, the more you will become better at it. Let's take driving a car as an example. If you cast your mind back to the day you took your first driving lesson, you will probably remember that it was a really scary, stressful but exciting day. How did it go? I'm guessing that if it was the same as most people, you stalled the car, crunched the gears, and drifted across the road as you concentrated on doing something else that the driving instructor told you to do. We needed practice and mentoring. A few people, very few, give up on their first attempt and then probably only because of a poor mentor. However, for the majority of us, we became determined to do better. And sooner or later we succeeded in passing our test, and many even on the first attempt. What about driving now? It may still be a bit scary, but at least you can recognise good and bad driving behaviour, and you change gears with ease – particularly if the car is an automatic, but I'm sure you get what I mean. And it's the same as dealing with sensitive issues: the more you do it, the easier it should become. But it does require you to step outside your comfort zone. There are two points here: the first is that learning new skills is a bit like learning new habits; and the second is that learning new habits nearly always requires us to step outside our comfort zone.

'In order to learn the most important lessons of life, one must each day surmount a fear.'

Ralph Waldo Emerson

Think back to anything of value that you have achieved in life: your degree/diploma from university or college, your marriage, your car licence, your ability to play a musical instrument, or any skill you're proud of. All of these skills and achievements have necessitated a certain degree of risk – the risk you might fail. And in many ways, this is part of value creation: if it had no value (intrinsic or extrinsic) then there would be no risk of failing – you simply wouldn't care if you were successful or not. In simple terms, risk creates value and vice versa. You cannot have one without the other.

Every one of you reading this has friends: some more than others. And some will be closer to you than the rest, but nonetheless you all have friends. And they all have one thing in common: they like you for who you are. In other words, you don't have to pretend or put on an act with them. For the most part, we can therefore be relaxed with our friends and enjoy their company. We can be ourselves. So, if your friends like you for who you are, there is a fairly good chance that others who don't know you will also like you for who you are. Conversely, we do need to be cognisant of the fact that some, a smaller number, may take a natural dislike to us too. It is the same way that we prefer to be with certain people than others. We naturally bond with people who are similar to ourselves – or facets of ourselves. If you agree with this then here's the suggestion: be yourself, be sincere, and step outside your comfort zone now and again. From a more practical standpoint in dealing with sensitive issues, I've found the following model to be very effective in instigating change from the other person.

SENSITIVE ISSUE

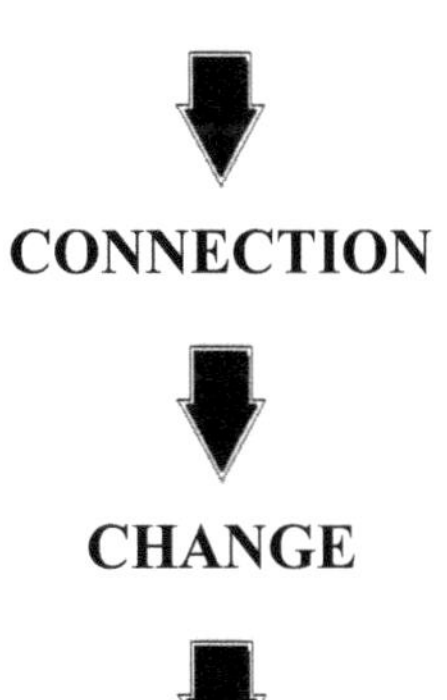

SUPPORT

As you would expect, some people are more easily upset than others, so it will be necessary to modify your approach based on the individual and what you have in common with them.

Golden Guideline for Giving Feedback on Sensitive Issues

Find something in common or a story you can share that will lead to talking about the problem indirectly. From there you can lay hints with varying strength in the hope that the other person will get the message. If they don't then you may have to be a little blunter next time.

Sensitive Issue:

The person has unpleasant body odour.

Connection:

"It's really hot these days, isn't it? I even had to buy an extra can of XYZ deodorant this month. What brand do you use? I find XYZ is really good value for money."

Change:

"In fact, there's a shop near my home that's got a deal with the second purchase at 50% off. Would you like to try it if I get one for you?"

Support:

"Oh hi, how's it going? I notice you seem to be coping much better with the heat these days."

Receiving Advice

We all receive advice, and for sure, not all of it will be good. Generally, if the feedback is good, then we are very happy with it. Often people only listen to the good bits anyway. However, when the advice is constructive criticism there can be a Pandora's Box full of reactions including: -

- I'm different from everyone else, so it doesn't apply to me.
- No-one understands my situation.
- They're describing the past. I've changed recently.
- Maybe, but I just don't care anyway.
- You really must have it in for me.
- The good bits are true, but the bad bits sound like someone else.

  And so on: the list is long.

What can I do to make sure everything goes as well as it possibly can?

Place

The first thing to consider is where the meeting will take place. If the person giving the advice is uncomfortable with the task, or they are simply evil and want to give you a hard time, they might select a place that puts them at an advantage, such as their home or their office. A true friend or a good manager will select a neutral place or somewhere you'll both feel comfortable. But it's not always possible, especially in a work context, and you may just have to put up with the place they choose.

Listen

And by this, I mean really listen. Of course, listen to what's said, but also listen to what's not said. Before this advice gets too esoteric, I should explain that we choose what we avoid talking about as much as what we do choose what we say. People will often run away from mentioning the full picture. They may hint at it, but perhaps because they fear adverse reactions from the listener or receiver, may just leave it at that. So, we need to tune in to how the person giving the advice is feeling. By doing this, we will be in a better position to see if there are other things we should ask questions about to get the full story.

Much of the time, the people receiving advice only listen to the 'good bits': the bits that make us have a warm fuzzy feeling inside. But this is a mistake, as is the paranoid approach of only listening to the negative elements. It's also a fine line between trying to extrapolate a bigger picture from the limited information given, and hypothesizing into the unrealistic. We need to get all the information and then rationalize it based on the situation and environment. Only then will we see what is possible to adjust for a better outcome. Ask questions to elicit the otherwise hidden or reluctant information.

Clarify

As much as the givers of advice may try to give factual and justifiable feedback, there will always be an amount of subjectivity. As a result, we have to filter out the facts from the opinions, and to do this we need to ask questions. For sure we hope that the answer will be what we'd like to hear, but we must also be aware that the answer may also not be. To ensure quality advice the receiver should always listen out for specific examples of activities or behaviours that exemplify the point being made. This is especially the case with constructive criticism because the listener often struggles to see what's wrong with the actions they've taken, or why the person is making such a big fuss of things. Simple, polite requests such as "Could you give me an example of ..., please?" is usually enough to get a clearer picture. Occasionally you might find this clarification-seeking question puts the other person on the defensive, especially if they are unable to provide a specific example. In this case you might like to help them by suggesting, "Am I right in thinking you mean ...?" Hopefully this will be enough of a prompt to help them. Alternatively, if you have a mean streak, you could just pause and wallow in the silence while you watch them squirm in the unease of being trapped into a situation they can't explain themselves out of. Avoid letting the mean streak out.

Keep asking

When you get an answer to the above clarifying questions, there is often a tendency to accept the answer at face value and leave it at that. Don't! Keep asking yourself 'why is that the case?' and 'Do I really understand what they mean?' You need to walk away from the situation with a clear picture of what you did well, what needs correcting, and a clear picture of how to go about it. Asking for clarification about an issue is excellent, but if you're not completely satisfied with the answer then probe a bit more.

You might find that what is given as the problem may just be a facade for the real issue which is harder for the speaker to articulate and is often to do with personalities and their clashes. And clashes of personality are like leeches in a jungle: they cling on until they've drained you, or had their fill, and then they drop off and leave you alone until the next time.

Get a second opinion

I have this sneaking suspicion that, judging from some of their inexplicable actions, some of the people on this planet are aliens in disguise. Yes, very tongue-in-cheek, but think about it: why do some people act the way they do? They can be totally irrational. For example, I know people who go to nightclubs in Indonesia to listen to music played so loud that they can't hear themselves think. They also breathe in so much second-hand smoke that it would be safer if they put their nose up a car's exhaust pipe. But the most bizarre are the people who seem to revolve their lives around other people's unhappiness. They go out of their way to create clashes of personality. However, there's a simple answer to personality conflict and that is to recognise that you have some differences, and let the other person know what type of person you are and why the differences occur. Then deal with it. Focus on the shared goals and what you do have in common rather than the personality of each person. There's also a more complex way: start your own company, then use your preferred method of personality testing and hire only the type of person you're likely to get along with. Bizarre? Yes, so realistically we have to accept that we are going to come into conflict with other people. Keep in mind that the irascible personality may be in ourselves.

As mentioned earlier – and worth mentioning again – we're all different and although some individuals will get very distrustful and self-protective, others may just shrug the problem aside. Whichever you are, follow the proverb at the beginning of this chapter: ask a close friend for a second opinion. Other people sometimes see things in us that we can't see ourselves; and it's useful to know these things because they affect the way people interact with us.

Keep it real

This refers to putting things into perspective. We all get criticised: no-one is exempt. Therefore, it would be a bit strange if we didn't. So why worry about it? There's really no need for any defensiveness. Admittedly there are better ways than others to give criticism (see above), but put whatever's said into context to help. See advice as a chance to improve.

Hopefully it will be presented as such. When people's nerves are on edge and they're wearing their personalities on their sleeves, there is a natural tendency for them to get defensive. Try not to, because it doesn't really help things. A key point here is that you don't have to accept or agree with the advice, but you do have to acknowledge that at least one person feels that way. If you feel that they are talking about someone else and not you, the onus of responsibility is then on **you** to find out more by getting a second opinion and reflecting a bit deeper on your actions and their rationale for mentioning it – keep it real.

Change

Easier said than done! For change to take place three things need to occur: realisation, acceptance, and desire. First, we need to realise that there is a better way of doing things, or that the current habits we have are not as good as they could be. Then we need to accept that it refers to us and not someone else. Acceptance, real acknowledgment that we could do things differently, is crucial to the last part, which is desire. Desire refers to the 'want to' element. You might even understand that things could be done a better way, and accept that you are not yet doing it, but without the desire to change, nothing will. Unless you're forced, but then the change is unlikely to become permanent or a part of the new you. It would be like forcing the proverbial square peg into a round hole.

Change can be good or bad depending on what you want for the future. Two important questions to ask are 1. What do you really want out of life? and 2. How will you know when you've attained it? If you ponder on those questions for a while you will hopefully see a path emerging. The path will, without doubt, change as you proceed on it. But the question is still 'will you change?', because change brings the unknown, and the unknown can be a scary place without desire.

Golden Guideline for Receiving Feedback

1. If you can, choose a place where you feel comfortable.
2. Really listen to what's said. And also listen to what they should mention, but avoid talking about.
3. Ask questions to make sure you understand what the real problem is. Get specific examples.
4. Keep asking until you've clarified in your mind what you've done and what you need to do; make sure you've got the complete picture and not just a facade of the real issues.
5. Ask friends you trust if there's any truth to the feedback you've received
6. Put things in perspective: everyone gets criticised, so there's no need to get defensive.

7. Acknowledge, even if you don't completely agree, then look at developing new habits.

'Ask for feedback from people with diverse backgrounds. Each one will tell you one useful thing.'

Steve Jobs

Summary

It is not always easy to give or receive advice. Both the giver and the receiver need to be aware of the fact that the information given, when acted upon, should be mutually beneficial. And effective communication is crucial to the outcome.

7. Developing and Using Emotional and Social Intelligence in Interactions

'Emotional Intelligence is the capacity for recognizing our own feelings and those of others, for motivating ourselves, and for managing emotions well in ourselves and in our relationships.'

Daniel Goleman, 1998

To explain what EI and SI (Emotional Intelligence and Social Intelligence) are I'd like to present 3 scenarios for you to think about, and I'd like you to consider how you would react in the given situations. Sit back, relax and picture yourself in the following encounters.

Scenario 1.

It was a rough night and you didn't sleep particularly well. You're also a little late. You go to make some coffee only to find that you have no filters left and you have to use the freeze-dried instant variety that you don't usually like. But you need a coffee. You are mentally juggling what the day has in store for you as you pick up your freshly-made toast, which then drops to the floor, jam-side down, of course. You reach to pick up the toast but in doing so you brush the coffee mug which then spills on the cat which has come to eat the jam on the floor. The cat screeches in pain and wakes your other half who comes out of the bedroom to see what's going on. He or she then starts berating you about being more careful. You decide to call it quits and give up on your coffee and breakfast and go to work. You are running a little late anyway, and you have a very important meeting first thing in the morning with your bosses. You get to your car and see that you have a slow puncture which you do not have time to fix by changing the wheel. You decide to risk it and drive out to the main road. As you get to the busiest junction you notice that the traffic lights are not working properly and they are changing extra fast on your side of the road. This is causing a backlog that's likely to make you miss your meeting. As you get closer to the turning, you consider that you might just make the appointment if you can get through the next time the lights change in your favour.

The lights go to green and the cars are going through one by one. You get closer. The lights then turn amber, but you are the next car to go through and you're going to make it.

Just then, out from the back of the queue, a purple Perodua with 'go-faster' stripes, fluffy dice dangling, and a mega-large exhaust pipe cuts you up and forces you to slam on your brakes and therefore wait for the whole sequence of lights to finish again before you can go through, almost certainly sealing your fate for missing the meeting. And as the ancient purple car passes you, the driver – a greasy-haired, spiky-eared, pimple-faced student – leans out of his window and laughs at you.

How do you feel?

What would you say?

What would you do?

Scenario 2.

You find the perfect present for your partner in a shopping complex. It's a bit on the expensive side, but you know he/she will really enjoy it – his/her birthday is tomorrow. However, when you get to the checkout the sales girl apologises and says the credit card line is down and they can only accept cash, but the store is willing to give an extra 5% discount on the item. You are okay with this as you need to get some more cash anyway, so you go down to the ground floor where the ATMs are.

It would seem that a lot of businesses are having the same problem as there is a long line of people waiting at both machines. To compound the problem one of the ATMs runs out of cash and that queue joins the other one at the remaining cash dispenser. And you quietly join the back of the line. The good news is that the queue is moving quite quickly and before you know it, you're the next in line to access the machine. The person in front of you successfully completes her transaction and takes her money.

As this happens you take out your ATM card in anticipation and hold it in your right hand. However, just as you step forward and raise your card to put it in the machine – at this point many readers think that the machine runs out of money, which is not the case because a greasy-haired, spiky-eared, pimple-faced student, with jeans hanging halfway down their bum, pushes your hand out of the way and inserts his card into the machine instead.

How do you feel?
What would you say?
What would you do?

Scenario 3.

You suddenly realise that you're running out of some medicine and decide to drive to the local shops to get some from the pharmacy. Unfortunately, it's also a busy Saturday afternoon and the parking bays are almost full. Nevertheless, as luck would have it a car pulls out just as you are driving up to the shops. Because you are just nipping in with your prescription, which is usually a very quick and simple affair, you decide not to put any money in the parking meter as you are able to watch the space through the pharmacy's window.

When you get inside the shop you see that they have a sale which has attracted a larger number of people than usual. There are also a couple of people waiting at the prescription counter. You make your way to the pharmacologist and hand in your request.

You wait patiently as the single counter staff deals with the numerous questions about the medicine they have just received. Eventually you are served and pay for your treatment in what seems only a matter of minutes. However, just as you step out of the pharmacy you notice a smartly-dressed, fresh-faced, young, and attractive traffic warden just about to fill out a parking ticket for your car.

How do you feel?
What would you say?
What would you do?

In the first two scenarios it's likely that you would get angry. Reactions range from mild annoyance to extreme anger with hand gestures and abusive language – the latter being more common than the former. In the second, this is often accompanied with physical aggression including hitting or pushing the student. In the third situation, people nearly always try to plead with the nice, attractive person not to give them a ticket, which sometimes works – even if they aren't so sweet.

Now consider three variations on the above, but ask yourself the same three questions: **How do you feel? What would you say? What would you do?**

For the first scenario, imagine the same situation, but instead of the greasy-haired, spiky-eared, pimple-faced student cutting up your car, it's a huge, bearded, aggressive man with a baseball bat resting on his dashboard. And he snarls at you. Would you react the same way as before?

For the second scenario, imagine that instead of the same greasy-haired, spiky-eared, pimple-faced student at the ATM, it is a little old lady with a white stick. Would you react the same way as before?

For the third scenario, imagine that instead of the smartly-dressed, fresh-faced, attractive person, it's a huge, bearded, aggressive man who is tapping the parking meter with his nightstick. Would you react the same way as before?

Our actions are dependent on the people involved, much more so than the location, conditions or the setting. How we react is the basis for our emotional and social intelligence.

In all three situations you would react differently. For most people, as these are extreme examples, the differences would be marked. As the situations decrease in severity, the amount of change in the person also decreases. Now I appreciate that we are all different and react in our individual ways to any changing circumstances. Nevertheless, the fundamental point I wish to make here is that we react differently to people, not to situations. You can take the same situation but put different people in them and we will react differently. In other words, our actions are dependent on the people involved, much more so than the location, conditions or the setting. How we react is the basis for our emotional and social intelligence.

Think of the last time you got angry with someone. It probably happens every day and possibly many times during the day. Now think of replacing the person you got angry with, with another person, preferably someone you are close to. Would you have got as angry with them as you did with the first person? The reality of it all is that we base our emotional reactions on who we are dealing with not what we are dealing with. Therefore, we choose to react in the ways we do, depending on who we are dealing with. And if we choose how we react, we are therefore able to modify our responses to get a better outcome from the interaction. By the same token, think now of the last time someone got angry with you. They did so because they thought they could get away with it. They chose to because they thought they could. It's quite a powerful thought, isn't it?

I define *Emotional Intelligence* as the understanding, management and use of one's emotions to increase the chances of achieving a better outcome in interactions. I define *Social Intelligence* as the same, but with other people's emotions. Although these definitions, on closer scrutiny, are likely to be flawed, they serve as very good working descriptions for take away point. If you can recognise when your emotions are starting to get the better of you, and you can manage them, and perhaps even change or use a more positive reaction, you will, without doubt, achieve a better outcome in any interaction. Similarly, if you know a person is acting in a particular way towards you because they think they can, then you are in a powerful position to change that by getting them to acknowledge it. Ah! Easier said than done I hear you say. And I would normally agree with you, but in this case all it takes is a little practice.

EI & SI in Writing

If I had a dollar for every rubbish email I've ever received I'd be very rich. The amount of idiotic, banal and clichéd messages out there in the ether is ridiculous. Yet there must be people out there who think they are sending something funny, friendly or informative. Often, they just aren't. In the workplace there are also a large number of rude emails that could make your blood boil. Have a look at the following email and consider how you would respond to it.

(9am) Dear Farishatul,

This is to inform you that I still haven't received the information you said you'd send last week. What's the problem?

You probably don't know this (or care) but I'm under a lot of pressure to finish my report and the deadline is latest by tomorrow 6pm when I have to present it to Chairman. And I need that information. If I don't get the information by lunchtime today you know I'll have no choice but to mention that you've held me up. Kindly send the information by lunchtime with an apology (if you have the courtesy) and the reason why you have caused this delay so I can mention this to Chairman.

How would you reply to such an aggressive and rude email? For many there would be the temptation to write a rude email back, but then you would regret it 10 minutes later, you really would, because once you've replied, it stays on the hard drive for a long time and can be retrieved for if needed. The key is not to rise to the bait. In other words, be as professional as you possibly can.

If I had the information, and the person I was writing to was the same grade or status as me (or lower), I'd reply as follows:

Attached is the information as requested.
D

If the person I was replying to was senior to me, I'd reply slightly differently:

Attached is the information as requested. Sorry for the delay.
David

Analysis

In both replies I would not waste time by beginning with 'Dear...' or 'Hi...' as I think it's unnecessary. This is the case with all emails providing that the time between them being sent is insignificant. At the end of the first example, I've simply put my initial to signify that the message has ended. In the second, I've written my full name for added politeness. Even so, I understand that (in some cultures) this may still be considered rude. However, I have no desire to respond with more than the bare minimum to people who are emotionally unintelligent and rude. I also think that giving further justification or apology as to why the information was delayed is tantamount to agreeing to be bullied in the workplace, which is unacceptable irrespective of rank or status. If the person was of a lower rank or status, it would be very tempting to let them have it, but that would be emotionally unintelligent too. It would just exacerbate the situation further and reinforce the bad feeling between us.

In the situation where I still didn't have the information that was requested earlier, I would use one of the following replies:

I'm currently waiting on XYZ/X department to finalise things. I'll send it to you as soon as it's ready.

David

Or for higher status or rank:

The information which you requested earlier is still unavailable. I'm currently waiting on XYZ/X department to finalise things. I'll send it to you as soon as it's ready. Sorry for the delay.

David

Analysis

In the first example I think it's probably acceptable to let them know why the information isn't ready, and importantly, that I'm not deliberately delaying things. I wouldn't apologise either as it might be considered an admission that the situation was my fault when it wasn't. However, if it was my fault and I'd just forgotten to send it I'd certainly apologise but would keep the reply as factual and professional as possible. People, particularly angry people, will always look for excuses to criticise your opinions, but they cannot do the same with facts.

In the second example, I've added more to the message which increases the politeness. The apology is added for the situation, not in any way an admission of guilt. It is possible to lengthen the message even further to make it even more apologetic, but given the brusque tone of the email sent, I'd be hesitant to make it any nicer.

Exercise: written application of EI & SI

Have a look at the following email and then consider how you would reply to it. You may assume that you don't have all the information as to whether all of the complaints are justified, but you intend to look into things.

Complaint Email

I have received very bad service from a Notverysurebank representative, Ms Sor Gui, from Dingly Dell branch. Overall, the experience I got was slow; she did not follow up my inquiries and did not call back as promised on at least 5 occasions. And it's very hard to get her to answer her mobile phone.

We have signed the Home Loan offer letter on May 8, but my lawyer complained to me that Notverysurebank only sent it to them 3 weeks later. I'm not sure if this is due to typical Notverysurebank processing time or late submission by the person in-charge.

There was also a mix up in the application for a credit card for myself and my partner. My instruction was clear that I would be the primary applicant for the card and give a supplementary card to my spouse. And my spouse would be the primary applicant for the Family and Friends card and then give the supplementary card to me. The result was that I received a regular credit card without the supplementary card, and a Platinum card for myself and supplementary card for my partner. The Family and Friends card was rejected. I requested her to address all my concerns last week and ask for the commitment to sort out all the problems by this week, but I did not get any follow up from her.

The joint account for the home loan. I followed up with Ms Sor Gui last week after I personally checked with the branch's office. To my surprise the officer who checked the record told me there was no joint account application at all. On the day we signed the offer letter (December 12), we filled in the application form and passed RM20 to open the joint account. I entrusted her to handle the account opening money but she still did not bother to follow up and give an update to me.

To me the overall service does not even meet the minimum requirement for a so-called professional relationship manager. Why is she even employed there?

Yesterday we tried to give her another chance and called her to get an update on the situation. To my surprise her voice mail mentioned that she would be away until the following Sunday. This is totally unacceptable. If she planned to be away for 1 week, why didn't she inform me earlier?

I need the above 3 items to be addressed immediately. I do not see any reason why the bank is not able to get this correct after 6 weeks.

Analysis

The first point to make is that the complaint was very badly written. Writing, or verbally uttering, a good complaint is a very valuable skill to learn, and one that should bring appropriate compensation. So, let's have a look at what's wrong with it. First, the message is emotionally unintelligent. A good complaint letter is factual in nature and avoids personal criticisms and emotional attacks. Secondly, make it as brief as you can without missing anything out. You do not need to keep repeating yourself several times to enforce a point. If you wish to highlight something, then add a short sentence to say so.

The general rule is that the more you demand, the less likely you are to receive.

Also try to stay on topic. While it's very tempting to mention everything under the sun, and vent your anger further by introducing other issues into your message, don't. All this will do is weaken your primary cause for complaint by diluting it within the other items you talk about. An additional error in the above complaint is that the writer makes demands of the bank. The general rule is that the more you demand, the less likely you are to receive. A much better way is to suggest what you would like as compensation, or what you would like to happen as a result of the complaint. This should be a main part of the complaint because the person you are writing to can't change the past, but they can alter the future.

Another area to consider when complaining is related to the notion of rank and status. Unfortunately, many people who still believe that 'the customer is king'. This is now a bit of a cliché. Customers deserve good service, yes, but the customer should also treat the server with the respect they would like to be treated themselves. The 'tone' of the message will vary slightly due to the perceived status of each person, but if you hold a higher status (and customers usually do by the very nature of being a buyer rather than a seller), there is no need to keep mentioning it: once is enough. Similarly, there is no need to use fancy language - large (bombastic) words, or complicated and rarely used phrases. The Golden Guideline for this type of communication is to keep it simple and succinct.

Finally, try to avoid pointing fingers at anyone. You may have to mention a person or people by name, but try to avoid using the term 'you' in an accusatory manner. All it does is make the recipient feel threatened and defensive which will result in a reduced probability that you will get what you want.

After you have thought out your reply, write it down and then compare it with the one below. Alternatively, you could just have a look at the answer and consider how it would differ in style with what you would have written.

Golden Guidelines for Complaining

1. Be emotionally intelligent: stick to the facts and avoid opinions.
2. Be as brief as possible: simple and succinct – nothing fancy.
3. Be practical: suggest what you'd like as compensation, but don't demand.
4. Be considerate: treat people the way you'd like to be treated.
5. Be level-headed: avoid 'you' with an accusation.

Dear Mr Noh Chan Suh

Thank you for your email to Notverysurebank of 10 January 2021.

Please accept our apologies for the unpleasant experiences you encountered recently

We are currently looking into this matter and we would appreciate it if you could allow us some time to investigate thoroughly. The relevant department will get back to you as soon as they have completed their investigation.

Once again, we apologise for any inconvenience caused and thank you for your patience.

Should you have any further queries at this stage, please feel free to contact me personally or one of our Customer Relationship Executives on 1800- Notverysurebank.

Yours sincerely

Analysis: the reply

Think back to the last time you verbally complained about something, anything. It might have been to your partner, friend, or even a stranger sharing the same experience. You probably felt quite irritated and wanted to share this frustration with someone. It happens all the time. But how did you feel about the incident one or even two days later? I'm pretty sure that you didn't harbour the same strength of anger that you felt at the time, because time changes things. It allows us to see things from different perspectives and therefore dissipate the anger.

Now think back to the last time you actually wrote a complaint email. Some of you may never have written such a message. In fact, a person has to be pretty angry to sit down and write a complaint after the incident has occurred. This is because time will already have been spent leaving the scene, getting to the office or house/flat, before you can write the first word. During this period the anger will have likely dissolved. Therefore, to write a complaint letter the person has to be very angry indeed. That's why it's so important to be as friendly as possible to negate any further wrath.

The opening line is short and references both the date the complaint was received and it thanks the reader for taking the trouble to write in. I know it seems a little strange to thank someone for complaining and being angry, but the answer is very simple: I would want to thank them for giving me the opportunity to address their concerns and then try to put things right so that no further customers are lost. And if by some chance it is the customer's fault in the first place, I will be in a position to keep them as a customer for life – providing I don't rub their noses in it.

I also avoid using the word 'complaint' as this would remind them that they had something bad happen to them in the first place. In other words, I want to move away from the negative aspects as quickly as possible and move on to the positive things **I can** do for them. And if there's nothing positive I can do for the customer, I would still want to minimise the negative elements and focus on what changes will take place to avoid any recurrence.

The second line apologises for the situation the person has experienced, but it does not admit liability as the situation is being investigated. It also offers hope for the future. This is the most important part: offering hope. With any reply to a complaint – justified or not – it's imperative to offer a better future. No-one can change the past by going back in time. And you can't undo what has already been done. Therefore, there is no purpose in dwelling on the mistakes a person or the company has made: it only serves to remind them of the bad service they received. However, what you can do is say that things will be improved in the future. We all live on hope: hope that tomorrow will be slightly better than today, and it's important to present this in your reply.

The next paragraph apologises again and praises the writer (thank you for your patience). This will hopefully make the reader feel as though we are taking the matter seriously and value his or her custom. The final paragraph provides a personal touch by offering the personal contact details of the person replying since it's important to make the complainer feel as though there's an individual that they can turn to if necessary.

Significantly, no compensation is mentioned. All that's offered is hope that a) they'll find out why it happened, and b) it won't happen again. This should never be promised, as what occurs in the future may be out of your hands. What could be promised is something like 'we will do our best to ensure that this incident does not happen again.' This promises you will try; it does not promise you will, because we don't know what the future has in store for us.

Another important point is that I have neither admitted liability nor apologised for each incident. I have apologised for the situation, not for anything specific. I have also avoided suggesting that it is the other person's fault (as it may well be) since casting blame in this situation merely adds petrol to the fire and enflames an already angry person.

Golden Guidelines for Replying to a Complaint

1. Thank the person for bringing the information to your attention.

2. Apologise for the situation, but do not admit liability.
3. Use your emotional intelligence and do not react to the criticism.
4. Show empathy, if you can.
5. Offer hope that things will be better in the future.

How Can I Improve my Emotional and Social Intelligence?

The next time you find yourself angry with someone, try to imagine another person, someone you quite like as a substitute instead and see how your emotions change. Consequently, by not reacting as much as you would have done, you will reduce the volatility of the situation. You will therefore make the communication less acrimonious and you will be able to work towards better solutions to whatever problems there are.

However, it does come with a warning. To absorb your feelings and change your reaction to people you dislike can cause frustration and stress. This is especially the case when you know you *could* shout at the person, or worse, because you know you have the authority to get away with it. However, you don't because you know it won't help the situation (in fact it would probably make it worse). Therefore, it is essential to ensure that you have a balanced outlet for any pent-up aggression and frustration such as sports, gym, outdoor activities, etc.

In all the literature on the subject, the research clearly indicates that developing a higher level of emotional and social intelligence is essential to achieving success in workplace communication. I would also like to add to this and say that it is imperative for working towards financial independence and career development.

Top Ten Tips for Improving Your Emotional and Social Intelligence

1. Reflect

Sometimes we may be unaware that we are projecting negative emotions such as anger, hate, condescension, envy and so on. To correct this, first be aware of other people's negative emotions and ask yourself what triggers these feelings in them. Additionally, when you are in potentially stressful situations reflect on the words and phrases you use and ask yourself, "How would I feel if I were asked that or spoken to in that manner?"

2. Listen

Listen to how many times other people use the phrases 'I should have…' or 'I have to…'. Then listen to how many times you use these same phrases. The first phrase is almost redundant because it describes something that you didn't do in the past, but it would have been better if you had. But the past is over and you can't change it, so why worry. Move forwards. The second phrase empowers things outside your control, so you are empowering others to control your life. Therefore, change these phrases to 'Next time I'll...' and 'I choose to...'.

3. Remember

You choose the way you react to people based on what you think you can get away with. Therefore, you could choose to react in a more positive way to get a better reaction. Ask yourself: What would happen if I didn't ... (shout)? or What would happen if I... (said something complimentary)? Also, in difficult situations, stick to facts rather than opinions as people are less likely to react emotionally.

4. Look

Whenever a situation starts to cause negative emotions, step outside your body and look at yourself from an outsider's perspective. This not only helps prevent the situation from escalating, but also allows you to see the other party from a third-person viewpoint. It may also allow you a greater insight into their opinion.

5. Remind

When you find yourself in a discussion which is growing in animosity, remind yourself of the things you have in common with the other person to maintain a good rapport with them. If necessary, return to those subjects to keep the other side from also getting too emotional.

6. Ask

In a difficult situation ask how you would feel if you were in their situation and then show empathy by reflecting those feelings. It is also a good idea, if you find an opportune moment, to ask the other side how they would feel in your shoes too (see the chapter on Negotiation & Persuasion).

7. Notice

Be aware of changes in the other person's body language, facial expression and voice. Understanding a person's body language (including facial expressions) is incredibly important as it gives a clear indication of what other people are actually feeling. It's very honest as body language happens naturally i.e. we don't think about doing body language (see next chapter for more details). Similarly, a person's voice pitch and tone will change as they go through different emotional thoughts or states. For example, if nervous or stressed, the voice pitch will rise. All these are clues to help you understand the other side better, and therefore be in a better position to change things.

8. Enjoy

Do something that makes you laugh or smile at least once a day. Life is too short and you need to enjoy it. Make sure you have something to look forward to with a life that offers you rewards you enjoy. And above all else, make sure you are comfortable with yourself. If not, it's time to do something about it.

9. Encourage

When people make suggestions, even seemingly silly ones, try to look for the positive in them and encourage other suggestions. Also encourage yourself to be as positive as possible. People like other positive people, so always try to look on the bright side of things even when they aren't necessarily going your way. It doesn't help to languish in negativity which achieves very little. And when people get emotional, let them – up to a point. We all have emotions and the best way to regulate them in an interaction is to put yourself in their shoes to try and understand why they feel the way they do.

10. Focus

Pay more attention to what you want rather than what you don't want. Moreover, try and make sure that what you want is given a deadline or a series of deadlines to make it appear more achievable. As with any good planning, make each step of the way small and very possible. If it's going to be tough to get to what you want, and the path there tedious, then focus on how you'll feel when you've achieved it. This will take the focus away from how hard it is to how good it will be when it's realized.

> **'Knowing others is intelligence; knowing yourself is true wisdom. Mastering others is strength; mastering yourself is true power.'**
>
> ***Lao Tzu***

Summary

Emotional and Social Intelligence are fundamental elements in communication. Without developing them you are greatly limiting yourself in your ability to communicate effectively. With a little practice you can use Emotional and Social Intelligence to manage the outcomes of your interactions better and achieve more from them. But also know what you want from every interaction too, as this gives you direction and focus.

8. Body Language: the secrets revealed

> **'I speak two languages: Body and English.'**
>
> *Mae West*

Body language is an incredibly important part of any face-to-face interaction. And it's also very honest because it occurs naturally – we don't think about doing body language: it just happens. As a result, it can be very revealing about how we really think about the people we're interacting with. It's therefore very important to discover a bit more about it, how we can minimise the barriers we present, and maximise our sociability.

A long time ago there was an experiment – call it research if you'd like – as to how we interpret messages. The academic paper was written by Albert Mehrabian *(1. Mehrabian, Albert. (1971). Silent Messages. Wadsworth Publishing Co)*. He wanted to see which was more important in understanding an utterance: the words used; the intonation of the voice that carries them; or the body language that accompanies them. The results they obtained suggested that body language was the most influential element. In fact, it became known by many as the 7%, 38%, 55% rule – the relative percentages to the above parts. However, I remember looking at a YouTube video of one of those celebrity motivational trainers leaping from one side of the stage to the other in a very excitable manner. And here lies the issue: I remember him leaping around the stage – the body language – and the entertainment value, but for the life of me I can't remember any of the points he was trying to make. Now, I'm sure he has good intentions, but on reflection it all seems so pointless, unless your sole function is to entertain. However, If the above percentages are accurate, I should have remembered so much more of the message. But I didn't, so let's look in more detail at how they arrived at the above figures.

I agree with most people in that an animated speaker is more fun to watch, and interacting with a person who gesticulates as they speak is generally easier to understand, but what is the function here? What is the purpose of the communication? If your objective is to entertain then yes, by all means jump around and wave your hands like a crazy person. But if your objective is to get people to remember something you say, then you don't have to behave like a windmill to do so. Simply make it interesting.

If words are so unimportant and 93% of communication is through tone and body language, I wonder why we even use them (words) so much. Just think, learning Chinese or Vietnamese should be so easy. But it isn't. You see, tone and body language can project primary feelings and attitudes quite well, but for complex issues and ideas you need words.

Further, Albert Mehrabian, is on record as saying that very little can be communicated non-verbally. Further, in 1994 he stated that his findings were of very limited application to general communication. So, perhaps it would be more accurate to say it is the misinterpretation of Mehrabian's work that has led to the myth that words play an insignificant (7%) role when communicating in public. The fact is this: words are tremendously important in communication. Just a few of them said at the right time can change people's lives. True, they can be enhanced by supporting tonality and congruent body language, but the bottom line is that words matter.

So, what about body language? Well, since you ask, it also has a very important role to play in supporting the words you use. Body language rarely lies as it is a subconscious action. We very rarely think of 'doing' body language as it happens naturally. However, if we try and learn a few body-language tricks to make ourselves appear more confident or convincing, then there is a great risk that we will confuse the people we're speaking to since it will quickly be apparent whether the body movement is genuine and supporting the message or not. For example, you think you should show compassion by consciously using body language tricks, but while your body may be doing what you want, your face will probably be showing your real feelings such as anger or frustration or vice versa. And what if you get it wrong? At a subconscious level people tend to believe the body language rather than the words you use. Consequently, your body should be congruent with the message you want to put across. Therefore, it is necessary to learn a little more about it if we are to be more effective with our communication.

With my own research, I have found that there are essentially four levels of body language: 2 conducive and 2 intrusive:

Conducive

1. Self-awareness
2. Social awareness

Intrusive

3. Associative approximation
4. Steering

The Four Levels of Body Language

1. Conducive - Self Awareness

Before you can use body language more effectively in your communication, it is necessary to be more aware of what your body is doing - *Self Awareness*. What is the little finger of your left hand doing now? Which direction are your feet pointing? Well, whatever they are doing, the real question is 'Were you aware of what they were doing or pointing before I asked you, or only afterwards?' Only you know the answer to this, but I suspect that you had no clue until the question was posed. And that's okay. So, to start on this body language journey, I would like you to be much more *self-aware* of what your body is doing in any presentation or communication. Are you folding your arms creating a barrier between you and the people you are communicating with? Are you bringing your hands up to your face a lot, which would show that you are uncomfortable with the situation? Are you shuffling your feet, which would indicate that you would like to quite literally walk away from the encounter?

First, we need to take care of our own body language to ensure that we are not sending any negative signals or creating barriers.

Every movement we make, and every expression we use, gives more information to the people we are communicating with. Also, because it occurs at a subconscious level, we are rarely aware that we are doing it. Therefore, first we need to first take care of our own body language to make sure that we are not sending any negative signals or creating barriers to the communication.

The good news is that it can become a very easy and quick habit to adopt if we consciously focus a little more on what our bodies are doing in interactions. Some suggestions for this are presented in the summary at the end of this chapter.

2. *Conducive – Social Awareness*

The second conducive level of body language is to be more aware of what other people's bodies are doing. By observing this we can build up our own portfolio of which movements relate to which thoughts and feelings. We are then in a better position to understand how others think and feel about our message, and the quality of their understanding.

This is perhaps the easiest habit to get into as people generally like to watch other people. We can see this every day at cafes and other public areas. In fact, whenever a loud voice is raised or there is a strong laugh, we instinctively turn our heads to look. A strong, but very common example of this is on the roads of some developing countries. I have personally been involved in traffic jams of monumental proportions when there has been an accident. But an accident on the **other** side of the road, and people just want to slow down to 'rubber neck'. For example, in Malaysia I have even seen people slow down to write the car number plate so later they can stand a better chance of winning the 4-digit lottery - the rationale being that the driver has had so much bad luck that there must be some good luck coming soon to balance out the bad. Madness, but there you are.

The next time you are travelling by public transport, or are in a shopping mall, or at a café, or even at work, observe people unobtrusively and see what their faces, hands, feet and bodies do in different situations. Then relate this to how you feel when you move in the same way or have the same posture. The chances are that you will, to varying degrees, generate the same feelings for yourself as the person you have been watching. Go on and give it a try: it's actually quite fun.

One small caution with this: I've called this a '*conducive*' approach as I believe that if you are more aware of other people's body language and what it represents, then you will be in a better position to understand them. However, one group of pre-university students took this advice a little too literally and went to the local coffee house, sat down and 'picked on' suitable targets and then jotted down in their note books the body reactions they saw, what they said, and the emotional element that accompanied them. And, quite rightly, this angered one customer so much that she walked over and asked them what they were doing. Therefore, I again emphasise the word ***conducive*** when developing your skills. Observe to gain knowledge, not to interfere or manipulate.

If you are more aware of other people's body language and what it represents, then you will be in a better position to understand them.

Below are some of my interpretations of other people's body language. Clearly, the situation in which the action takes place determines much. For example, having your hands in your pocket while listening to someone could indicate boredom, but from the perspective of someone about to give a speech it would probably indicate nervousness. Likewise, folding your arms in front of you is usually a sign that someone feels defensive with what you are saying, but they might also be cold. As a result, the following table is a general view of the way people feel when they interact with one another, be it one-to-one, a small group, or many. And in isolation, without the relevance of what the other bits of the body are doing, should only be taken as a simple guide to get you started on building your own understanding. Building your own portfolio is far more crucial.

Body Posture	Simple Interpretation
Hands in pockets	Wants to hide/Nervous
Wringing Hands	Feels uncomfortable/Nervous
Locking hands behind back	Subservience/Nervousness
Shuffling feet/ fidgeting a lot	Wants to leave
Hands straight down sides	Nervous and overly formal
Face touching	Unease/ Nervous
Hands on hips	Arrogant/ Over confident
Folded arms	Defensive
Hands leaning on something	Casual/ possibly covering nervousness
Crossed legs	Defensive or Cautious
Arms clasped behind head	Arrogant/ Over confident
Hands forming a loose triangle	Relaxed/ Thoughtful
Eyes looking up	Exasperated or Thinking
Eyes looking left	Mentally searching memory
Eyes looking right	Mentally creating
Eyes darting from side to side	Not admitting something/ Nervous

Eyes looking straight ahead	Visualising/ Controlling
Pacing	Self-absorbed

3. *Intrusive – Associative Approximation*

There are also two intrusive elements to body language: Associative Approximation, and Steering. Taken largely from research involving NLP (Neuro-linguistic Programming), they are *intrusive* because they can be used to alter the perceptions of the person or people you are speaking with.

Perhaps the best example of associative approximation is to ask you to remember the last time you were in a group of strangers – it could have been at a concert, a party, or just a gathering. Now ask yourself the following questions:

Did you feel more comfortable with one person more than the rest?

Did you feel more uncomfortable with one or more of the people you were talking with?

Most people have been in this situation several times and the chances are very high that you answered 'Yes' to the first question, and probably the second too. The reason for this is because, in the first situation, you had similar body postures to the person you felt more comfortable with. There is a considerable body of research which suggests that ***if you are***

like-bodied, you are like-minded. In other words, you may not have been aware of what you were doing with your body posture, but it was probably very similar to the other person(s) you felt most comfortable with.

This, in turn, sends a signal to each other's subconscious to say that 'Hey, this person I'm talking to is thinking the same way I am, we must have similar views and opinions on other subjects too.' These messages then get filtered through to the conscious mind to say that you like the person.

Because body language is complex and takes place (for the most part) at a subconscious level, we don't know that we are 'doing' body language. We just feel naturally more comfortable with the other person. Conversely, if there is an uncomfortable feeling from the other person it is probably because they have either a very defensive or opposite posture to you.

> **I call it intrusive because by deliberately moving into the posture of the other person, we are attempting to manipulate the other person's thoughts in our favour.**

We can exploit this principle if we wish to by moving into the same or similar posture of the person we are talking to. By doing so we are using conscious thought to influence the other person by communicating with, and affecting, **their** subconscious. This is why I call it intrusive because by doing so, we are attempting to manipulate the other person's thoughts in our favour. We are therefore being insincere with our body language and using trickery to win over the other side.

It is also a very risky tactic and can lead to severe reactions and repercussions if discovered.

I remember the time I conducted training at a large merchant bank and another trainer from a different organisation was delivering a workshop at the same place - next door in fact. We met up at the end of the day to have a chat to compare ideas and try and establish if one of us was undercharging the client. Immediately I sensed that something was not quite right and I felt as though I was being scrutinised. The reason for this feeling was because he was deliberately trying to copy my body language. He had very quickly and very obviously started to mimic my body posture to try and establish a (false) rapport. He did this to encourage my subconscious to feel more comfortable and therefore put me in a position where I would be more inclined to reveal information which I otherwise wouldn't.

Therefore, out of interest, I decided to see how far he would go to mimic me. Slowly, at first, I moved my body into increasingly awkward postures to which he dutifully followed. He therefore gave me the impression he was unaware that I knew what he was trying to do. I swung my leg - he swung his leg; I rubbed the back of my neck - he rubbed the back of his neck; I leant against a chair - he leant against a chair, and so on.

He finally seemed to grasp what I was doing and abruptly ended aping my movements. And the conversation died a death. It was poor communication. Perhaps, I should have let him carry on, pretended not to notice and focussed on the positive elements of the interaction rather than the negative. However, I am really not interested in someone who wishes to try and get inside my head and manipulate my thoughts, ideas and opinions through tricks rather than through logical reasoning. Are you? I am also not interested in the person if this is their way of interaction. I like real people – I may not agree with them all the time (and they with me), but I will respect their views if they believe in them. And I honestly believe this is the case with most people.

Being sincere and genuine with people is by far the best way forward for any communication.

Perhaps it was wrong of me to tease the other trainer this way, but I am sure he will be much more cautious before he mimics again. The result could have been much worse. For example, how would you feel if you knew that someone was deliberately trying to influence or manipulate you through deception; that they were using dishonesty for their own gain? I am fairly sure that most people would agree (with me) that they dislike the idea. Being sincere and genuine with people is by far the best way forward for any communication.

4. Intrusive – Steering

The second intrusive element of body language (and the fourth level) is *'Steering'*. It involves using your own body language to *steer* the other person's body language into a more beneficial posture for you i.e., you are altering their body language with the intent of using their new body posture to affect the way they think. Let me share with you an interesting example of how this works. I was window-shopping in Singapore and came across a tailor's. I wasn't particularly interested in a new suit or shirt and neither was another gentleman walking just ahead of me – it was a busy street. The instant the gentleman peered in the window, the shop owner came out to greet him, and he did this by extending his hand to shake the hand of the potential customer. And the customer, without thinking, also extended his hand because it's the natural response. The shop owner then had the potential customer in his grasp to try and convince him to purchase something. This shopkeeper was rather insistent, and refused to let go of the customer, literally taking them by the hand into their shop. A veritable 'human' Venus Flytrap.

This particular *technique* even forms the basis of a school-kid game of trying to get the other person to look foolish. It goes like this: the protagonist makes the movement of extending their hand which is then retracted as soon as the other person also extends their hand. This leaves the latter with their hand held out and with the knowledge that they have been controlled by the former. Yes, it doesn't make much sense now, but we were kids.

And because we are so conditioned into this reflex action, it takes considerable will power to not comply with extending our own hand. In fact, later that day (interestingly also outside another tailor's), the shopkeeper rushed out and extended his hand expecting me to do the same. I can honestly say that the urge to conform was very strong, but I managed to resist and it was the shopkeeper who was left with his hand extended in mid-air. "Aren't you going to shake my hand?" he asked. "No, thank you." I replied, and walked on. Was I being rude? Perhaps. But when someone does this to manipulate you, I think it is perfectly acceptable. I don't like feeling manipulated, and I'm guessing that you don't either.

A more positive use of *Steering* is to try and relax people who are being defensive. An example of this is when you are with a group of people and you've touched on a sensitive issue and hit a raw nerve. You can generally tell when this happens as the body language of the person you are speaking with changes.

You may find that they cross their legs or fold their arms to create a barrier towards you. You might also see the shuffling of feet almost as if they wish to walk away. Or face touching. All these are signs that they are unhappy with what you have just said. Therefore, to change this negative reaction to you, you can *steer* their body language by leaning **slightly** closer to the person you're speaking with and using open gestures with the palms of your hands facing up. And smiling kindly. By adopting this somewhat avuncular posture and manner, you can alter the attitude of the people you are communicating with. They will, without knowing why, relax the physical barriers they had previously and pay more attention to what you are saying. They will, in effect, become more open with you because you have used your body language to steer theirs and therefore their thoughts and feelings towards you.

A quick note here on personal space when communicating with people. You will find that personal space is culturally defined and it will vary depending on who you are communicating with. Generally, those people who come from nations where they live quite far apart from each other will usually require a larger personal space e.g. British, Germans, New Zealanders, etc. Conversely, those people who live in close proximity to each other – Hong Kong comes to mind – require less personal space. The point is that you can make the people you're communicating with very uncomfortable if you invade their personal space. In reality this should not happen providing you have developed the second level of body language – ***Social Awareness***. You will find that the people you are communicating with will very quickly form some sort of barrier between them and you (probably with their hands and arms), or they will start to move away from you.

Unfortunately, not everyone has developed this type of sensitivity and I remember waiting patiently in an Air Asia queue with an Indian gentleman with a protruding stomach standing behind me. As soon as the queue moved forward, he would move so that his stomach rubbed against my back. After a very short time I became annoyed about this infringement of my personal space. I tried to make light of the situation by turning around and asking him if he was intending to propose marriage to me, and if not, could he move slightly away. The look of apoplectic horror on his face clearly gave me the answer to the proposal question, but this was quickly replaced by puzzlement - he had absolutely no idea why I had mentioned this. To him, he had done nothing wrong and was perplexed by this lunatic passenger in front of him. His personal space was clearly much smaller than mine.

From the perspective of interactions, we can use the principle of *steering* if we want to get the attention from the people we are talking to, but may not be listening. The two primary ways of doing this are to use silence, and to move closer to people.

If, for example, you have been invited to talk to a group of people at a social function of whom some are more interested in their incoming iPhone messages than you, you should move more towards them while speaking. Their subconscious will then recognise you are there as an intrusion to their personal space and send a warning message to the conscious mind to ask *'Why is he or she here?' 'What's going on?'* It has the effect of extending an invisible hand to lift the person's head towards you. Silence is also a very powerful tool to get attention, and this will be dealt with in the chapter on Negotiation and Persuasion.

So, what should you make sure you do?

Body Posture

In communication, and especially if you are meeting someone for the first time, it's a good idea to maintain a neutral body posture. This is obtained by having your feet slightly less than shoulder width apart with an even balance on both legs. However, a note of caution here for taller people. If you stand with your feet too close together it has the effect of making you look a little unsteady and unsure of yourself. If you stand with your feet too far apart it will look like an exercise class. The best thing to do is look in a mirror for a posture which suits your frame. Another very important point to remember with stance is to avoid 'hiding' behind anything such as a desk or other furniture, or a bunch of papers, or anything that acts as a barrier between you and the person/people you are speaking with.

Hands

Your forearms should be approximately 90 degrees to the rest of your body with your elbows slightly away from your waist. Your hands should be open to allow you to gesture with your fingers and palms. Do not put your hands in your pockets, behind your back or wring them together so tight that the knuckles turn white and the fingers red.

Gesture

Use gesture to support your points. Avoid thinking too hard about the gestures you are doing and let your subconscious do the thinking for you. After all, body language is something we do best naturally. However, the general rule for gesture size is to keep your arms within a circle made with your fingertips and arms without moving your elbow. Be aware of any annoying mannerisms you have such as clicking a pen, pointing fingers, cracking knuckles and so on, and try and get rid of them.

Eye Contact

Look at people, but don't stare. They should feel that you are talking directly to them, at least some of the time. If you want to engage their attention and want them to buy into what you are saying, you should look at them. Similarly, if they are interested in you, they will look at you.

There's a bit more about the eyes you should know, because the eyes can tell you an awful lot about what the person is thinking and feeling at the time of speaking.

If you look at the face above and the eyes move to the left, studies in Neuro-semantics have told us that people do this when they being creative, and therefore may be lying. Conversely, when people look to the right (as you are facing them), we know that they are accessing the cerebral cortex i.e. memory and are therefore probably telling the truth. There is some evidence that the reverse is true in left-handed people, but the above is mostly universal. Eye movement can be further divided into segments depending on how we think.

Following the diagram on the previous page, if the person answers a question or talks about something and his or her eyes go up and to the right, we know that they are trying to recall a visual memory. This is likely when a person responds to questions such as 'What is the colour of the shop that's nearest to where you live?' If the eyes move horizontally then we know they are thinking about the sound of something. To the question 'What does the tune of your favourite song sound like?' the eyes are likely to move horizontally to the right. However, to the question 'What sound does a cat make underwater?' the eyes are likely to go horizontally to the left as they create an answer. The slight exceptions to this are when the eyes move down to the left as they answer. This indicates that they are thinking kinaesthetically i.e. about touch. This would happen in response to a question about what it feels like to put on damp socks. And if they move down to the right it indicates that they are thinking about the sound of their own voice or talking to themselves.

There are further variations on this. For example, people may initially look to the right and then roll their eyes to the left. This would indicate that they are trying to remember, cannot, and so try to give an answer that they think you'll be happy with. Then there is the slow blink, which people subconsciously do when they know they're about to be trapped in a lie and they try to mask the eye movement. Then there are those who do not move their eyes at all. This is because either they don't have to think about the answer, since it's already in their mind, or they are deliberately trying to control their eye movement to avoid being caught in a lie.

Although there is substantial evidence to support these classifications, it will take considerable practice before you can use this information effectively. Nevertheless, once it becomes a natural observation to help you digest the communication, it can assist in understanding if there's something the other party is leaving out, or an area you need to enquire more about. This is why in interviews people always manage to ask you the questions you'd least liked to be asked. After all, they do say that the eyes are windows to the soul.

The above explanation is relatively straightforward and a good start to your awareness of body language. However, for further and more detailed explanations of eye movements and their meanings, I'd urge you to check out eye accessing cues on-line, or have a look at a good NLP book.

The final point regarding this chapter on body language I recommend is one of the hardest: smile. An appropriate smile is very disarming and friendly. The only problem is that the more nervous you are, the harder it is to do. But it is possible, at least now and again. And it works wonders.

> **'Our bodies are our gardens – our wills are our gardeners.'**
>
> ***William Shakespeare***

Summary

Body language is complicated and could warrant a book in its own right; however, be sincere and your body will follow. If you don't like the people you are talking to, your body will reflect this. So, make sure you focus on the positive elements of the interaction. Below is a summary adapted from my book on presentation skills.

The Dos and Don'ts of Body Language

DO	DON'T
Be natural	Over emphasise
Stand evenly balanced, upright and relaxed	Shuffle or sway from side to side
Have your hands free-floating above your waist	Put your hands in your pockets, on your hips, behind your back or mangle them
Stand in a place convenient to you and the person you're speaking to	Hide behind anything
Express ideas of size, shape, movement	Fiddle with papers, pens, glasses, etc
Show emphasis, and use counting gestures	Use repetitive gestures (e.g. smoothing hair, adjusting tie, tugging ear)
Make appropriate eye contact	Stare or look away as soon as people look at you

9. The Law of Attraction: being positive

'You create your own universe as you go along.'
Winston Churchill

The Law of Attraction asserts that we attract moods, emotions and people who are similar to ours. In other words, if we are miserable then we will attract other miserable people and make others miserable. Similarly, if we are happy, we will attract other happy people and make others happy too.

Being positive alone is not enough: you have to act on the wonderful opportunities it presents.

The Law of Attraction is very simple and you most certainly don't need to go on one of those expensive workshops to find out about it - unless, that is, you need a motivational kick up the bum. What I would recommend though, is a little healthy scepticism regarding its claims. They suggest that you can become rich by following the Law of Attraction, and to a limited extend I'd agree, but you have to work at it. It is no use just thinking about being rich, then writing a cheque and putting it on your mirror. Or buying a lottery ticket and winning - that simply doesn't happen, or we would all be driving around in Bentleys or Rolls Royces. If you follow the Law of Attraction, you are likely, although not certain, to come across more possibilities which may enhance your wealth, some by a lot and some by a little. The point I want to make here is that being positive alone is not enough: you have to act on the wonderful opportunities which positivity presents.

You can apply being more positive to all aspects of communication. Here are four golden guidelines you should always try and use with speaking and writing:

Four Golden Guidelines

1. Avoid negative vocabulary such as 'don't, isn't, can't, won't, not', and 'No'.

2. Always put what the reader/listener wants to read/listen to before what you want to write/ say.

3. Avoid trigger words that would inflame an already difficult situation such as 'complaint, fault, hate, problem', etc.

4. Always add benefit whenever you want your reader/listener to do something for you.

All of these can best be exemplified with a true story.

I was invited around a friend's house recently for dinner. The meal served was roast chicken with stuffing and vegetables: delicious! The hosts were very gracious and even their daughter was on her best behaviour. However, when it came to the meal the spoiled child ate all the chicken and stuffing, but left all the vegetables. Of course, the concerned parents wanted the child to eat the vegetables to get a balanced diet. And the child had pretty much the opposite view. Unfortunately, the fretful mother then said the worst possible thing she could.

> ***"If you don't eat your vegetables, you can't have any ice-cream."***

Not only was this a very negative statement, it could also be perceived as a threat. It also managed to contradict everything that should be used (the four Golden Guidelines). Naturally the daughter wailed and screamed and ultimately refused, and left the table in a huff. Now you could argue that the parenting skills need addressing, and I'd agree with you wholeheartedly, but for the purposes of this chapter, let's just focus on the verbal communication used.

If we follow the first Golden Guideline: ***Avoid negative vocabulary such as 'don't, isn't, can't, won't, not', and 'No'*** and change the sentence the mother said (*"If you don't eat your vegetables, you can't have any ice-cream."*), we end up with the following:

"If you eat your vegetables you can have some ice-cream."

This is much better. It's exactly the same message, but it's delivered using positive language as opposed to negative bullying. But there's still a better way of conveying the message and that's to apply Golden Guideline #2: ***Always put what the reader/listener wants to read/listen to before what you want to write/say.*** By doing this we end up with the following message.

"You can have some ice-cream as soon as you've eaten your vegetables."

Again, this is a vast improvement on the first message, and a good progression on the improved one above. By approaching the message this way, you cater to what the person wants to hear first before you put what you want to say. It has the effect of making them more amenable to your suggestions because they have the part they are interested in still in their mind. You may have even found yourself saying to people "hold on, let me finish" to suggestions you make even when it's for the listener's benefit. This is simply because you phrased it the wrong way round and they jumped to their conclusions about the meaning of the message.

Nevertheless, there is still a better way and that's to follow Golden Guideline #3 as well: ***Avoid trigger words that would inflame an already difficult situation such as 'complaint, fault, hate, problem', etc***. If we apply this, we now get the following:

"You can have some ice-cream as soon as you've finished your meal/cleaned your plate/eaten your dinner."

You might argue that this difference is negligible and that we're now just playing around with words. But word choice is very important – you ask any successful salesperson. The effect it has in this case is to take away any remaining mental barriers to comply with the request. It therefore makes it easier to agree with.

To apply Golden Guideline #4, ***Always add benefit whenever you want people to do something for you,*** is a little more challenging. Particularly in this case as the benefit has already been added in the form of 'ice-cream'. However, it's still possible to add further benefit by mentioning why the parents want the child to eat the vegetables in the first place, such as the following:

"To help you grow up to be healthy and smart you should eat a healthy food. And you can have some ice-cream as soon as you finish your dinner."

Applying this to more general communication is actually easier. For example:

"You'll have to take it to one of our service centres to get them fixed."

Becomes

"To keep repair costs down we ask customers to get them fixed at one of our service centres."

"We don't give out names and addresses of customers over the phone."

Becomes

"To protect our customers' privacy, we ask customers to obtain the addresses by either writing in or popping into one of our centres."

Although the sentences become longer, and from a writing perspective that's an important consideration, it is far more likely you will get the person to comply. You see a lot of people aren't really interested in your side of things and often miss the point of why you're asking them to do something in the first place. They just want what they want as fast as possible. For example, if you ask someone to fill out a form for you, they are likely to whinge, and perhaps chide you as to why they have to do it when they see it as your job. But if you add benefit, the situation takes on new characteristics, for example: *"To speed the process up, please fill out this form with as much information as you can."* By adding an often-obvious benefit, you're more likely to achieve your goals.

Applying the Law of Attraction to Communication

'The meeting of two personalities is like the contact of two chemical substances; if there is any reaction, both are transformed.'

Carl Jung

If a headless chicken could speak, I would imagine that its favourite phrase would be "I should have done this/that".

A lot of people actually run around like headless chickens after they've said or done something, even though there is nothing they can do about the situation after the event. It's all in the past, and how ever hard you try, you can't change the past. These people are afflicted with focussing on the negative things that have happened. The irony is that because they dwell on these negative elements, they are doomed to repeat them in a kind of self-fulfilling prophecy sort of way. And this is what the Law of Attraction refers to. However, we can also apply it to get a more positive outcome.

Try an experiment. The next time you're in your local supermarket, or if you're brave, go up to someone in the street, and smile at them. The result is usually that the person will smile back and they won't even know why. We are conditioned to it – it's a learned behaviour. It's the same when someone holds out their hand – you generally reciprocate because we associate it with a positive outcome.

The point of all this is that the Law of Attraction means one positive action nearly always results in a similar response. And if we want someone to not do something (which is a little strange anyway), or perhaps remind them to avoid doing something, then the brain processes the positive first and then changes it. For example:

"Don't think of a car, and don't think of the colour of that car." What happens, of course, is that we immediately think of those items: we cannot 'not' think unless you are very gifted.

Instead of "don't be nervous when you go to that job interview." or "don't worry", we should probably be saying *"I'm sure you'll do well in the job interview."* to have more of an impact.

Let's take this concept a little further. If you want someone to do something, it is far better to lead them by supplanting ideas in their sub-conscious rather than try and force them.

People these days tend to be on the selfish side, particularly when it comes to bargaining over an expensive purchase or negotiating an agreement. For example, you can see the true colour of people's character through the way they drive. Will they let you into the main flow of traffic at a junction? Will they speed up to close the gap when they see you indicate to move into the fast lane? These days, people tend to be interested for only two reasons: 'What's in it for me?' and 'Do you know me?' The latter is wonderfully exemplified by the Zig Ziglar quote 'People don't care how much you know, until they know how much you care... about them.'

Your message can be delivered in many different ways. For example, if you want people to attend an event you are promoting you might have the following information regarding the function:

- The event is at the Grand Ballroom, Royal Hotel
- Begins at 7pm for drinks
- Pre-dinner speech by the host
- Dinner at 8pm
- Post-dinner message by Chairman of the Organising Committee
- Hand out of gifts – event ends

There are, of course, many permutations to putting this message across. For example, a perfectly good way would be to order the message chronologically as it is above. Alternatively, you could change the order to highlight certain elements depending on who you are addressing. For example:

Dear Mr (or) Mrs/Ms X

You are invited to a complimentary dinner on us at the Grand Ballroom in The Royal Hotel. Drinks will be served at 7pm sharp and dinner will commence at 8pm following a welcome address by (Host). There will be a short post-dinner message by the Chairman of the Organising Committee, following which a free gift will be handed out to all those who attend.

There are many parts to this message which uses the power of the subconscious to address the reader. The first is the use of the personal pronoun 'You'. You could equally write the first sentence 'We would like to invite you to...' However, we should

ensure that the reader (or listener) feels as though the message was catering directly to them – a kind of personal touch. Too often the personal pronoun 'We' is used at the beginning of messages which reflects that the person delivering the message is thinking more about themselves or the organisation they represent rather than the addressee. However, by this slight change of pronoun, you begin to talk to the subconscious of the person to say 'I care'. And this gets filtered up into the conscious mind as a message of friendliness. Of course, you don't want to use the 'I' and 'You' approach if the message is negative. For example, 'You failed to pay the parking fee on time. You must pay the fine by X' is an aggressive and threatening message. In this case, it would be far better to use the passive voice and get rid of the 'You'. The result is something like 'Because the parking fee wasn't paid on time, the fine must be paid by X.'

Golden Guideline

Use 'I' and 'You', but only use them when the message is positive.

For example, *"I'm happy to tell you that you've won the lottery."* However, in some cases you can also use 'I' and 'You', even when it's bad news. For example: *"I'm sorry to let you know that you've been unsuccessful with your lottery ticket."* Nevertheless, as a rule stick to 'I' and 'You' only when it's positive.

Let me put it in a different context. Have any of you ever experienced a situation where you've tried to contact someone by phone only to have your call answered by an automated answering service? I have and it can be hugely frustrating. The last event was to try and get through to my travel agent.

The machine welcomed me and then asked me to select a number from a large array of choices. After this I was told to 'wait for a few moments' while I was connected. Then I was welcomed again and asked to key in a 13-digit membership code, which I didn't have handy, so I was told to press the 'hash' key when again I went back to a list of options. And in-between all of this was the most grating, annoying and thoroughly idiotic Pinky and Perky type tune playing on the background. Eventually I got through to someone, and although angry at having to put up with all the unnecessary rubbish before I got there, I felt relieved that at last there was a real person on the other end of the line that could probably help me. The point here is that people need to feel connected with other people. It was true before and it's still true in this social media age. People are important and this should be reflected in the way we communicate with each other.

If we get back to the message above, you'll notice that I've not chosen a chronological order because I wish to emphasise some parts of the message more than the rest. This is because my goal is to attract my readers to attend. And what I think they and most people are interested in is something of value, but free.

The beginning and end of your message, whether spoken or written are the most powerful parts: particularly the beginning.

However, if I was representing The Royal Hotel (for example), I would re-phrase the paragraph to begin with 'The Royal Hotel would like to invite you to...'. You see, the beginning and end of your message, whether spoken or written are the most powerful parts: particularly the beginning. This is the main reason I've finished the paragraph with something positive – the free gift. It's something I think the reader will keep in their mind, and also something to try and keep them from departing before the Chairman's speech.

Exercise: Try putting the following information into a coherent and positive sales pitch

1. You supply the best air-conditioners in the business
2. Your prices are higher than your competitors
3. There is a promotion currently running – the main purpose of the message
4. There's a 20% discount on new air-conditioners
5. The promotion is until the end of the month
6. To get the discount, customers have to trade in an old one
7. There's a 30% discount if the old air-con is one of yours

If we go back to the Golden Guidelines earlier in this chapter, we can arrive at something like the following:

Up to 30% off a New Coolair Air Conditioner

Coolair is currently running an exciting promotion that will discount up to 30% off a new air conditioner when you trade in your old one. We supply the best air conditioners in the business, which is reflected in their slightly higher than average pricing. This promotion lasts until the end of the month, so hurry down to one of our stores to check out our top-quality air conditioners. If your old air conditioner is not one of ours, we will discount 20% of your new one but if it is, we'll increase the discount to 30%.

Analysis

The title attracts interest because of the 30% discount, so there's no need to repeat it in the first line of the main text.

Instead, I'm putting the company's name first as I want immediate brand recognition before I mention the discount again. I then mention that they are the best in the business before the only negative thing about the message – the high price (more is mentioned on this in the next chapter: The Law of ***Fatal*** Attraction). I've put the negative part of the message in the middle deliberately because I want to minimise its impact by smothering it with positive points. The next sentence, which tells us about the promotion duration and urges the reader/listener to action, is fairly neutral. I then end with a reminder of the most positive point: the discounts i.e. the message I want them to take away.

But, doesn't everyone write like this these days?

Not always. And I also think there's something still missing. It's what I call 'Connection Quality'. This refers to making the message more approachable and believable. The above message comes across as a little cheesy, clichéd and tired.

Golden Guideline

You have to believe in your own message, and you have to be genuine in the way you put your message across.

Now have a look at the same message but written in a more approachable style that connects with the reader.

Coolair is currently discounting up to 30% off new air-cons. Just trade in your old air-con for one of our new ones and instantly get 20% off your new one. And if the old one is one of ours, we'll increase the discount to 30%. We know our price is slightly higher, but we believe we're the best in the business. And we're ready to prove it to you. This exciting promotion will only run until the end of the month, so please don't leave the decision to buy a new one too late.

This message works a lot better because it moves away from formulaic rhetoric i.e. it comes across as more genuine. It was written with an almost chatty style that allows the reader to get a feel for what the writer is saying. It has a 'personal touch' that's been missing from communication ever since sales gurus tried to pigeon-hole people into one homogeneous group so they could apply one sales formula after another. These days being different is recognised more and appreciated for what it is. And this must be reflected in the way we communicate our message to people.

Before, customer service personnel used to be told to 'put a smile in your voice'. Even if this was over the phone and the person at the other end can't see the smile, they could sense a greater degree of warmth in the message. The person listening the then likely to react more positively. It became the same with writing.

But there's a problem with this because, if you're having a bad day, you really don't feel like smiling.

Therefore, to stand the best possible chance of your message being favourably received, or more favourable than it would otherwise, you need to be positive when you write or say the message. When this is difficult, either because you're having a bad day, or you've been asked to write something that you disagree with, look for the positive parts of the message that you can support and agree with.

There was a humorous cartoon I saw once which said something like 'People like sincerity – learn how to fake it and you've got it made!' The point here is that people respond well to genuineness, providing they can see that ultimately what you do and say is geared towards their benefit. But you can't fake it well enough to fool all the people all the time. And this is the biggest curse: you can't even fool most of the people for any of the time.

What's happening is that we are now used to being bombarded with advertising from every medium, especially on social media. So we are becoming more aware of what's genuine and what's not, because we've got a lot more information to compare and filter than before. While advertising executives search for the next creative idea which will shock, intrigue or delight, the rest of us are processing what we've already seen and comparing it with what we are presented with. There are only so many new ways of presenting information. Until the next tech breakthrough comes along, we are reaching a saturation point for the presentation of information. At this juncture, it becomes harder to 'pull the wool over someone's eyes'. We've seen it all before. We are more aware and more sensitive to how other people think.

We like the idea that our thoughts are private. But are they really? We have been subtly educated through media to the clues regarding our words, intonation and body language and what each of them mean. You may feel that you are individual and that only you think a particular way. However, many others are going to be thinking the same way too from the conditioning wehave been receiving over time. Therefore, more and more people are aware of what's genuine and what isn't. It's not just among married couples or long-term partners or best friends. The person on the street is a more educated person, not necessarily so in terms of formal qualifications, but in a more astute capacity for processing the information they've been given.

How does this affect our day-to-day interactions?

Say, for example, you walk into a restaurant/bar and you bump into someone you haven't seen for a while. As soon as you 'place' them i.e. you remember where you last saw them, you adjust your conversation, your choice of words – and your body will subconsciously react too. Generally, you will be polite because the social situation determines it and there is a high chance that you will disingenuous; there will likely be an element of falseness to your discourse. Naturally, you are unlikely to treat them like a leech even though they may have the properties of one. And you'll make polite conversation even though they smell like a hamster, have the fashion sense of a Barbie doll, the intelligence of a sea cucumber and the conversational ability of a root vegetable. But you'll still be 'nice'. Sometimes being disingenuous is important for us to all get along.

Focus on the commonalities, not the differences

However, coming back to the main point of this section. Although, it is sometimes necessary to be disingenuous, the bottom line is that people do respond well to genuineness – that is, once they feel comfortable with you. However, to reach that level of comfort it may be necessary to temper your barefaced honesty with restraint.

If they know I'm insincere should I still continue with the pretence?

You focus on the commonalities, not the differences; the things you agree with, not the ones you don't; the things you share, not the discrepancies. A tough task, I agree, but it works. If we take the example of a person with bad halitosis. I honestly believe they would appreciate your genuine comments providing they felt comfortable with you, you were sensitive with your delivery, and they can see it is for their benefit – it creates a sense of hope that things can and will be better in the future (check out the chapter, The Law of Fatal Attraction).

During an interview on national radio in Malaysia about business writing, I was put on the spot at the end of the programme with the question "What skill or quality makes for the best sales person?" I replied that the best way to convince people is to use people who have first sold the idea, product or service to themselves i.e. convinced themselves of the value and worth of the item. Coming back to a sales perspective and the air-conditioner examples, you will see that testimonials are crucial to convincing people. Having other like-minded people say positive things about a product or service is a powerful influencing factor. It convinces a potential buyer that if other similar people like it, then I should too. Moreover, what makes a product or service great is not what the product is or where it's made: it's what exists in the customer's mind. The rapport created between the company (its staff) and its customers can make positive impressions not just possible, but a reality.

To look good on the outside, you need to feel good on the inside

In communication then, we should really follow the belief that to look good on the outside, you need to feel good on the inside. A well-known person with seven very interesting habits once suggested that we should carry good weather around with us. What he's suggesting is that we react badly when we're having a bad day and react better when we're having a good one. He then links this to the idea of weather and recommends we carry around our own good weather. We should create the good weather ourselves by being more positive about things. Good advice, but easier said than done.

Reality check: we can't always feel great about the person we're communicating with. And we can't always create 'good weather' feelings. Sometimes it requires a chemical kick-start such as a glass of wine or several. And I think it would become incredibly irritating to be with someone who is on cloud nine (happy) all the time. But there is something else we can do instead. The difference is to be as genuine as possible with your communication i.e. make sure you believe in the message you are sending. It is really a question of imagining the person you are writing to is standing in front of you.

And when communicating face-to-face, because your body language will probably give you away, the answer is to focus on the message rather than the person. If you feel you're going to be negative about the message, then think about the information in the chapter on EI & SI again.

'Attitude is a little thing that makes a big difference.'

Winston Churchill

Summary

Following the four Golden Guidelines at the beginning of this chapter will certainly help you to structure any message better. You can further improve the impact of your message by adding a sense of sincerity and genuineness, which is possible by asking yourself if the message reflects how you feel about the subject.

The Law of Attraction (The Secret) is really very straightforward and quite effective. You really can alter your situation by adopting a more positive approach to life. And when things don't go to plan or the unexpected happens, try to see the positive aspects of what's left. It really doesn't matter if you fail at something providing you can take the learning from it and make sure that you do whatever it is differently next time.

10. The Law of Fatal Attraction: being positive about being negative.

'It takes but one positive thought when given a chance to survive and thrive to overpower an army of negative thoughts.'

Robert Schuller

The Law of Fatal Attraction

Unfortunately, many people cling needlessly to negative ideas and feelings so as not to raise their expectations, or attempt something they may fail at. These are avoidance-type people. When they try something new, they'll make it so difficult that there's no loss of face at failing. Conversely, there are over-confident people who have an equally distorted reality. These are over-achievement types and they will convince themselves, and anyone else who listens, that he impossible is actually possible. Optimism is a good thing, but it needs to be tempered with a healthy dose of reality. I think this is where most people seem to misunderstand the Law of Attraction. For example, writing a cheque for $1,000,000 and sticking it on your bedside mirror is not going to bring that money to you, but the desire and focus on that as a goal will provide increased opportunities for you to get closer to it. So, let's be real for a moment and recognise the fact that it is not always possible or desirable to be positive all the time. You may, on occasion, be asked to convey bad news, but bolster the message with a happier ending, or at least wrap the negative message in linguistic cotton wool to minimise the impact. For example, you may be organising an event or trip and you have to let some people know that they can't attend due to over subscription. Or you run a small company and you have to let someone go, which will mean more work for the rest of the group. In fact, most 'change' messages involve doing more for less, even though there may be greater opportunities too.

To look good on the outside, you need to feel good on the inside.

For the most part, it is not an easy task to convey this type of announcement as it is human nature for most people to be suspicious of change and look for the negative elements which will affect them. This is why it is crucial to minimise the elements the listener or reader may perceive as negative as soon as possible and highlight the positive outcomes of the change.

Recognise the fact that it is not always possible or desirable to be positive all the time.

Unfortunately, so many people are consumed by what I term the Law of Fatal Attraction. This states that when people know they have a 'bad news' message to deliver, they become so obsessed about hiding it that quite the opposite happens, and it ends up being highlighted. When the announcer gets to the bad news, you can often notice that he or she takes a small step backwards, or their body language shifts to indicate unease. If they are holding anything, they are likely to bring this closer to their chest. There may also be some face touching, again indicating unease. And all these messages are registered by the listener. Some of them are filtered through to the conscious mind, which highlights this part of the information as essential, therefore the term 'fatal attraction'.

Minimise the elements the listener or reader may perceive as negative and highlight the positive outcomes of the change.

Perhaps worst of all, they leave the bad news until the end of the announcement, almost as if they are trying to avoid having to say it, or pretend it's not there. But this only highlights it because the beginning and the end of the message, whether spoken or written, are the most important parts, and the listener/reader naturally focuses more attention on them.

So, what should we do?

The answer is fairly simple, and I like to think of it as going to a Japanese restaurant with a person who has never tried sashimi (raw fish). On one hand, the chef could cut off a piece of raw salmon, dump it on a plastic tray and slap it in front of you. For the person who is eating raw fish for the first time, it would appear very unappetising. Conversely, if the chef cuts nice slices and displays the fish in an attractive way, has other sculptured vegetables around the fish with waves of shredded 'daikon' (Japanese radish) as a backdrop, and has all of this on a beautiful plate, then there is a good chance that it will appear delicious. In other words, it's all about how things are presented.

Say, for example, you have been asked to give some bad news to an applicant for a job at your company. I call it the 'Bad news sandwich' and it goes something like this:

Thank you. Nice, nice, nice.
Bad news.
Nice. Opportunity. Thank you.

When you put this into an email, it might look something like the following:

Dear Mr. Customer

Thank you for applying for the position of .....

We feel that matching the right individual with the right job is essential, so we consider applications very carefully. After reviewing your experience and background, we have decided to pursue other candidates whose qualifications more closely match the needs of our position.

We have saved your information in our database and may contact you if jobs matching your qualifications open. We also invite you to visit our website XYZ to apply online to other jobs that may interest you. New opportunities are posted regularly.

Again, thank you for your application and we wish you all the best with your current job search.

Analysis

This is a well written message, but to put it bluntly it is still a 'get lost' letter. It literally begins with 'Thank you' in the first and last paragraphs - albeit with the word 'Again' used as a linking device - and has the 'get lost' part somewhere just before the middle. Perfect.

What about longer and more complex messages?

When you have longer messages with more complex variables (e.g. an announcement to the supervisors and junior management in your company about the merging of two departments), the structure of the message needs careful manipulation. However, it still follows the rationale behind the 'get lost' letter above. The following example is taken from my book on presentation skills, but it can equally be applied to both written and spoken communication very effectively.

The situation is that senior management have decided to merge two departments together, and you have been tasked with delivering this message to the staff concerned. The reason the management have proposed this is to enhance efficiency and minimise work duplication and staff costs. Unfortunately, part of this efficiency drive is to take some staff and deploy them elsewhere, while others will be made redundant. Admittedly, it doesn't sound like there can be anything good for the staff in this, but as the presenter you have to find something.

Firstly, you have to create hope. Without hope, the staff will have nothing except your head on a plate when you deliver the message. With ***hope***, they will be concerned that it will affect them, but hope that it will be minimal and therefore accept the news better.

Secondly you need to look for positives. The reason for the merging of the departments may look a very selfish act on behalf of the management. However, the management would not exist without the staff and vice versa – it's a symbiotic relationship. Let's say that the first positive could be opportunities for staff to move to other departments, learn new things and therefore get more from the job (and out of life). Perhaps there is the possibility of a promoted post or two. Let's also say that the merging will also allow a release of funds to upgrade some of the tech hard and software to increase efficiency.

Then there is the question of redundancies. Redundancies can also be opportunities although the staff involved may not think so at the time. I have met many people who, in retrospect, have stated that getting fired was one of the best things to happen to them as it literally forced them to start thinking about their future from a fresh perspective. Nevertheless, at the time when you deliver your message, you can bet it will not be seen this way. This is probably the most negative part of the presentation and you would want to minimise its impact as much as possible.

You start putting your notes together and come out with the following main topics and points that the senior management have instructed you to mention.

How would you order the following information?

a) The HR department will be conducting training seminars on C.V. writing and job interviewing techniques to help those staff who are affected to be better prepared to enter the job market place again.

b) There will be redundancies. You don't know how many yet because not all the information is available to you, but you will inform those who are affected as soon as you hear anything.

c) The new space available will allow for better working conditions, and the management has agreed to the building of a new pantry.

d) A number of staff will have new computers with the latest flat screens to ease eye strain. Some staff will have to make do with existing hardware until the budget for next year is approved.

e) The accounting and finance departments will merge. This will ensure increased efficiency and therefore lead to a more stable future for the company.

f) An overview of the company and what has led to the current efficiency drive.

g) There is a strong possibility that the company may introduce a performance-based bonus system in the near future – probably early next year although you don't have all the details yet. This will be in addition to the existing salary increase agreed by the management last month which will come into effect from the beginning of the next quarter.

A Common Approach (but not the best)

Often, the person delivering the message will organise their material so that they get the listeners on their side as soon as possible – this is particularly the case with a hostile audience. In other words, they start with a general opening and then try to allay any of the listeners' fears by mentioning all the positive elements, leaving the 'cost' or negative points until the end. The hope here is that the audience is less angry when they finally hear the bad news and therefore take it better.

It is an interesting theory, although I think there is a better approach. Have a look at the following order which was suggested to me when I presented this exercise and see what you think.

f) I'd select this as the opening as it's a general overview; a sort of scene setting which may also allow for any latecomers to catch up.

g) This is probably the best news available and not really related to the redundancies, so you have them thinking in a hopeful and more positive frame of mind.

d) This is also a positive point for the staff although not all the staff will benefit initially. It will still be possible to word this so it appears more positive than negative.

e) This is where the main news really begins. Ultimately the increase in the company's financial stability is good news for the staff, although some of the listeners in the audience will already be considering some of the ramifications of this merger.

c) This is also very positive and can only really be mentioned after saying that there would be two departments merging. It may get the sceptics who were wondering about any potential negative consequences of the merger back on my side.

a) The idea of training is positive, although there are still many factory and semi-skilled workers who are wary of professional courses as they see it as a threat to their status quo. However, it does dovetail nicely with the last point about the redundancies.

b) This is the point that I would try to get through quickly so that, hopefully, the impact of the bad news is minimised and all of the earlier positive points remain in the audience's minds. By leaving this until last, I could also finish to let the staff consider the possible consequences on their own rather than ask too many difficult questions that I wouldn't really have all the answers to yet.

However, I believe this approach would be a mistake because it leaves the audience with a negative take-away from the presentation.

A better approach...

f) I'd still select this as the opening since it's a general overview. It sets the scene which helps put things in perspective so the audience will understand why changes are necessary.

e,b) I would try and combine these two points. I probably need to say the main change (the merging) before the results of this (redundancies – negative; greater company stability – positive). And I would probably mention these sub-points in the following order:

- **greater company stability**
- **merging of the two departments**
- **redundancies**

The audience will be a little anxious to hear the main message, so put yourself in their shoes before presenting it. Bringing the negative point out into the open at this stage is much better than leaving it until the end where it could fester and mutate into something worse than what it really is. You are the messenger only, so deal with the issue rather than run away from it. Now minimise the negative impact.

a) This point reaffirms that the above change will take place: it eliminates any uncertainty. Most importantly it's a positive point that offers hope to those who may be affected and will consequently start to erase, albeit minimally, the impact of the bad news.

c) This is another positive point that further weakens the impact of the bad news. It gets the audience's minds processing this new information and therefore thinking less about what has been said.

d) Although this point has positive and negative elements, it starts to move away from the news of redundancies and therefore further weakens the link between the speaker and the bad news.

g) This is very good news and it's the message you leave the audience with i.e. a positive one. People have selective retention (see the next chapter) and research shows that there is a greater tendency to remember good news rather than bad news. You are offering hope for a better future which is tremendously important when giving any presentations with bad news as one of the main aspects.

We can also use the analogy of writing a medium to long report or proposal. If you remember the last time you looked at one of these documents, the first thing you did was probably read the executive summary. If, and it's a big if, you were motivated, you would then start reading the rest of it. However, I remember reading that on average, less than 20% actually read the whole report. Interestingly this percentage increases or decreases depending on whether the document is shorter or longer than anticipated.

At the end of each section there is usually a summary, and at the end of the report there are usually recommendations. Sometimes the recommendations are even put first with the rationale following. Following this there is a paraphrasing of the recommendations at the end. The point here is that reports, proposals and presentations have a lot in common when it comes to giving bad news, particularly when it comes to the organisation of the material. As with any proposal or similar document, emphasise the benefits when the audience is most alert or has a greater ability to digest information i.e. at the beginning and at the end of the message.

I have also called this approach 'Building a Straw Man'. In other words, you should build up an (insubstantial) argument against your views or suggestions until it looks quite credible, and then take a couple of matches (supporting arguments for your idea or proposal) and quickly burn it down.

Building a straw man serves three main functions: it shows you have considered most, if not all, of the alternatives; it increases the credibility of what you say (or write); and it also emphasises the plus points of your line of reasoning. It's not always necessary to use it, but it's very effective when you do.

> **'One can overcome the forces of negative emotions, like anger and hatred, by cultivating their counter-forces, like love and compassion.'**
>
> *Dalai Lama*

Summary

When talking to a group of people, or writing a proposal or a report, start as positively as possible and end as positively as possible. If you have anything negative for your audience or reader, you can minimise the impact – if you want to – by putting it fairly early on in the delivery or document, or hiding it in the middle somewhere. You can then erase the negative effect of it by finishing with positive points. These good points erase the bad ones due to a lack of memory retention on the part of the reader or listener.

11. The Only Guide to Negotiation & Persuasion You Will Ever Need

'Let us never negotiate out of fear. But, let us never fear to negotiate.'

John F. Kennedy

Nearly every book on negotiation begins with the same idea. We negotiate every day and in all facets of our life. It could be dealing with the boss, the spouse, the kids (especially the kids), the car mechanic, or just about anyone. However, the question I wish to deal with in this chapter is: Can we approach all negotiations the same way? Is it realistic to negotiate the price of a fake designer T-shirt at the local flea market the same way as you would your colleague at work, or with a friend about where to go for a drink?

You could argue that the principles are the same, so why not use the same approach? Actually, if you did, you'll probably be more successful than you would have been otherwise – at least you'll be approaching the negotiation having previously thought about it. However, remember that, to varying degrees, negotiations are different and each one has its unique characteristics. Particularly because each person we deal with is slightly different from the last. Therefore, change the words and phrases used to cater more to the person you are dealing with, and couple this with the ideas and guidelines in this chapter, and you should be well on your way to being more successful with all negotiations that come your way.

Let's start with human interaction since there are a number of choices to approach the negotiation from.

APPROACHES TO INTERACTION

Escape - no deal	Compromise - lose/lose
Surrender - lose/win	Win/win - fantasy
Conquer - win	Synergy - success

Escape: When the negotiation involves sensitive issues or personal problems, many people would rather run away from the confrontation. And it may be that some of the so-called problems will solve themselves over time anyway. However, if the situation is likely to repeat itself, then the conflict may get worse and become more difficult to solve. Should you 'nip the problem in the bud', or 'let things sort themselves out in the fullness of time'? My advice largely depends on the type of person you are. And, more importantly, the type of person you're dealing with. If they are the type that takes things to heart quickly, you need to be a bit more cautious in your negotiations, in other words don't rush into things. However, one over-riding point is this: if you can see that the situation is likely to get worse the longer you leave it, then address the issue as soon as possible.

- **Surrender:** Sometimes things are just not worth fighting for because the cost of winning is too great. For example, other people may not always be right - actually they are often wrong because they may not have your product or service knowledge - but is there any value to proving them wrong? If, for example, a customer is complaining about a faulty item, it might just be better to smile and replace it rather than negotiate. So much business is done because of word of mouth, and a flourishing business can fail quickly, especially given the immediacy of social media. In more general communication, if your spouse wants to do something their way, but you feel your way is better, it may be more prudent to just surrender and let them do it their way. In other words, it may be foolish to do anything other than surrender as to argue the point may prove a costlier outcome. However, this does set a precedent, and if you give in once, you will be expected to give in every time. My advice is to make sure you fully appreciate the value of the issue or item you're negotiating for. Then it's easier to decide whether to force the matter, or recognise that it's just not worth the stress, hassle or friendship.

- **Conquer:** If you have the authority power to get your way, it can act as an excellent kick-off point to get things started. It can also act as a short-term fix to an immediate problem. However, you create a loser, and losers usually have low commitment to the outcomes of the discussions. In terms of a negotiation, you might like to push the discussions harder and harder until you get everything you want, but you also have to look at the cost in friendship, goodwill or future loss. For example, you may very well be able to squeeze even more discount because the store owner is a friend, but you have to put yourself in the other person's shoes to see if it's likely to impinge on the relationship you have. Therefore, you have to be very clear of the value of what you are negotiating for. And if that value is worth more that the relationship you have with whom you're negotiating, then by all means go for the kill – especially if you know you won't have to deal with them again. But if there is likely to be another negotiation in the future, then bargain wisely to include the feel-good factor for the other side too: no-one likes to be thought of or feel like a loser.

- **Compromise:** This is probably the most common strategy in human interaction, and ironically most of its advocates think of it as creating a positive outcome. In fact, they often confuse it with a win-win situation. Yes, it usually makes the interaction easy and quick, but the actual outcome is that both parties half win and half lose: neither side is truly satisfied with the solution. Further, when 'ego' enters the discussion, it can turn worse i.e. into a straight lose-lose negotiation. Compromise is a quick fix, but not really what someone should have in mind as their desired outcome before entering a negotiation.

- **Win-Win:** When people say they achieved this in a negotiation, I usually have an inward smile because it's as rare as hen's teeth. So, let me ask you an honest question for an honest answer: How often does the negotiation principle of 'Win-Win' ***really*** happen? And even if, on the rare occasion you feel that you've achieved it, isn't the 'Win-Win' defined in your terms? For example, I met one financial advisor that insisted they always got a win-win outcome. But the truth was that all they were really interested in was getting their clients to invest as much as possible through them. A clearer example was the time an acquaintance bought a new car. The dealer negotiated hard as did the customer. The salesman agreed to cut his own commission on the vehicle he was selling and he sold the car. Initially the customer thought that he had 'won' and achieved the better deal. But it turned out that the dealer lied about his commission and still received the full amount because the sum that he reduced the price by was within the amount that the company was discounting the car in the first place. So, perhaps this negotiation could be described as win-win; but is it really, because the dealer could have discounted the price even further. The dealer was the more experienced negotiator and got what he wanted. 'Win-Win'? Not quite, but close. I term it a 'Symbiotic' negotiation.

- **Symbiotic**: This is the term I refer to when we seek an ideal outcome. This usually means you 'win' all or most of what you set out to get. The approach is usually constructive and results in quality solutions. Unfortunately, it can be more time consuming in the short term than the other solutions above, but you are more likely to get the outcome you require and allow the other side to feel good about it. It requires high levels of confidence and awareness, and above all, thought and preparation. Try using the following advice.

The Before Bit

This is split into two sections: the mental approach; and information gathering.

The mental approach

Your mental attitude is crucial to the outcome of any negotiation. For example, if a boxer were to approach a fight thinking he might lose then the chances are that he will – the self-fulfilling prophecy. You have to believe that you'll be successful even if the odds are stacked against you. However, I think it's necessary at this point to mention that it's imperative to keep your approach based on reality. Positive thinking is good but it's very 1990s and very rarely works without a good dose of reality to accompany it. You also have to approach the negotiation from a functional perspective. In other words, you need to keep negative emotions out of the equation. Become practical, clinical almost, but at the same time, show interest in the other side. You need to separate your feelings about the people from the problem you wish to negotiate. If you like the person and bring this attitude to the negotiation, you are more likely to give away too much. Conversely, if you dislike the person then you are likely to get angry quicker. If you are aware of your emotions you are in a better position to manage them. Keep the atmosphere positive and focus on the situation. You should still focus on the person, to look for clues in their body language, facial expression, choice of words and so on, but in an emotionally intelligent way.

Separate your feelings about the people from the problem.

Information gathering

The other 'before bit' is about getting as much information as possible. Then you'll be more prepared which, in turn, means that you'll have a greater chance of reaching a deal closer to your ideal outcome. In particular, you need to find out what their real interests are and get behind the surface of the negotiation to find out what people really want. It's a little bit like the difference between features and benefits. The feature of a training course on presentation skills would probably be standing in front of the class to practise presentations; the benefit would be to increase your confidence when speaking to an audience. A feature of a negotiation is to discover the interests of the other person so you can have something in common with them. The benefit is that they will feel more 'in-tune' with you and therefore feel more comfortable. This is likely to result in them being more generous with their offer. This is described in the literature as 'interest-based negotiation'. It contrasts with 'positional negotiation' where one or both sides fix or anchor to a price, figure or percentage, and then proceed to try and defend it. For example, the following is a positional negotiation I recently overheard in a night market in Kuala Lumpur.

"How much does this watch cost?"

"180 Ringgit lah!"

"That's far too expensive, I'll give you 90."

"Cannot lah! Watch very good for you; 165 can ok?"

"Look, the most I'll pay is 120, coz I know that's what they cost in Bangkok."

"You handsome man what. You can afford ah, got waterproof some more. 150."
"Here's 130. Take it or leave it."

"Cannot lah. 150 good price. Me no cheat you. You buy no buy I don't care."

Tourist walks away and calls "130". Vendor says "Okay, okay, you win 140 can."

Alternatively, if the buyer had followed an 'interest-based' approach, he or she would have avoided asking the price until the conversation revealed something they had in common. Make small talk, ask questions, and get to know the person a bit more. Yes, I agree it takes more time than the 'positional' approach, but it is so much more likely to lead to a better price (or deal). Then, once you have established something you share – a feeling, an idea, an interest, a desire – you should be able to see if you know some information that might be of use to the other side. Do you have something to trade? This could be information, access to another person who could help with what the vendor is looking for, or just simply an idea that they could use to their benefit. This information can then be traded towards trying to get a better deal. You never know, perhaps their information or the people they know may be of further interest to you too.

You may not think you have much in common with a market seller, but you never know until you explore. You may have the same interest in cars, fashion, food, or places you've visited. And even if, after exploring, you still find you have absolutely nothing in common, you are still likely to get a better deal because you've made the effort to get to know the person better. And that will make them feel more comfortable with you.

Preparation is always a good idea for most tasks, and in negotiating, it's crucial to get a better outcome.

Preparation is always a good idea for most tasks, and in negotiating, it's crucial to get a better outcome. In fact, the 'power' in power negotiating is described in the literature as the 'Best Alternative to a Negotiated Agreement' or BATNA, and although the concept is a little dated now, it's still an excellent exercise to go through before you actually sit down at the negotiating table. Essentially, it's a series of questions you should ask yourself to find out what you would be happy to accept should the deal fall flat. What will you do if you can't seem to get the deal done? What would you be prepared to give up to get the most of what you want?

For example, imagine two people get retrenched and they both look for new jobs. The first person looks through the papers and finds the ideal job: good salary, hours and conditions. She writes off to the company and manages to get called for an interview. The second person also sees the same job and applies. She too gets called for an interview. However, rather than put all her eggs in one basket, she looks for more jobs, and comes across two other posts she would be reasonably happy with: one has a great salary but the location and conditions are not that good. Another job is in a wonderful location and the hours are great, but the salary is not so good. So, she writes off and gets called for an interview for these posts as well.

The second person goes to one of her interviews and is a little nervous, but in spite of this still does quite well and later hears that she's been offered the post. It's not exactly what she wanted, but okay nonetheless.

Then the day of the interview comes for both people chasing their dream job. Who do you think is likely to perform better in the interview? The answer is the second person, because she will be less stressed, knowing that she already has a job offer, and she has another interview after this. Sure, you could argue that the first person will be all hyped up and raring to go because so much more is resting on the decision for her. However, while a certain amount of stress is a positive thing, the amount produced at an interview is not.

The real skill in negotiating: creating and then removing the smallest possible slices from what you want and making them appear like massive concessions to the other side.

What the second person did to reduce her stress, therefore giving her brain space to think about her answers, was to create BATNA i.e. next best alternatives. She already had a job offer in the bag, and another interview to go to – if she wanted. Even if she hadn't been offered the first job, she would still perform better because she had alternatives. And it's the same with every negotiation you enter into, be it the place to go for dinner, or the proposed design of a new supercar. For sure you won't be able to have a number of completely new designs up your sleeve when you pitch the idea to the board, but you should have thought about variations on the theme you are presenting. Think of it like a slice of cheese. You'd like the whole piece, but you may have to shave off a small amount to please the other side. Therefore, the real skill in negotiating is creating and then removing the smallest possible slices from what you want and making them appear like massive concessions to the other side.

So, how do you get these alternatives (slices)? The answer is very simple: spend a bit more time before the negotiation takes place to answer as many of the following questions as you can.

- What are your options (fallback positions – slices of cheese) if the negotiation doesn't go the way you've planned? Put them in order of priority?

- What are you likely to have in common with the other side?
- How easy/difficult is it for you/them to find a similar product or service elsewhere?
- Have you asked creative questions about your and their strengths, weaknesses/problems?
- What emotional benefits are the other side looking for?
- Are your emotions, pride or ego getting in the way of the facts?
- What is the minimum you're prepared to accept; and what's the most you think you can ask for without getting laughed at?
- What makes the other person tick; what kind of person are they and how will they approach the negotiation?
- Is there anything the other side would like outside the immediate negotiation that you have influence over? Are there any people you know that could influence the other side?
- What are you or they really buying or selling?

With the last question, you need to really think creatively as to what the item you are negotiating for represents to you. For example, if we were all logical beings, we'd all drive the same car, have the same washing machine or eat the same food. But we don't. The reason for that is we interpret things differently. Many people will buy a car based on what it looks like without any thought to the engine or performance whereas another person may do the exact opposite. It's mainly because the car represents different things to different people. For some it's simply a means to travel from A to B, but for others it's a lifestyle statement. So, if we come back to question 10, we need to be sure in our minds what the item we're negotiating for means to us.

Finally think where the meeting is going to take place. You may not have a lot of say in this, but if you do, select somewhere that you feel comfortable. The chances are that if you feel at ease, you will negotiate better.

The During Bit

If you've done your homework, the 'during bit' should be relatively easy. Certainly, there are always exceptions. But in reality, people are hardly likely to lunge across the table waving their fists wildly. People are, in fact, relatively predictable.

Definitely you will want to make a good impression, so you greet each other and engage the other side with some small-talk to get to know each other a little better. You will also want to make the discussions factual and non-opinionated so you can move towards a beneficial conclusion. And naturally you will want to find something in common: something you share and can talk about. You will also want to listen more than you want to talk. But the question is: How will you get what you want? How can you influence them? My recommendation is to try some or all of the following:

Ask the other side what they would do in your position

1. **If you were me:** This is my personal favourite when the negotiation gets tough and neither side wishes to make any concessions. Essentially it refers to asking the other side what they would do in your position. For example: "You know my situation regarding delivery times and the price I'm constrained to, and also the leeway I have with the extras I can offer, so what would you do in my position?" If nothing else, it reminds the person to see things from your perspective and, you never know, they may be able to come up with a new idea that you hadn't previously considered.

2. **Pause:** I consider this to be the most powerful negotiating tool ever, but also one of the most difficult to execute effectively. It's one of the reasons that good presenters can make good negotiators because both require a good exploitation of pausing. It works like this: we communicate via turn-taking, so you speak and then I speak, then you speak and so on until the end of that particular conversation. This is also very similar to a negotiation: you make a question or a statement then you expect me to reply to it. However, if I pause, an uncomfortable silence exists which the other side will wish to fill. In other words, they may offer more

information that you can use, or may concede something they weren't planning to so they can fill the silence. You also find this with presenters. Rather than pause to let the audience process the information or to create impact with a point, they start uttering 'ers' and 'ums' (which have no meaning) just to fill the silence – to make them feel more comfortable in a stressful situation. In a negotiation, pausing can mentally throw the other side into disarray and leave them scrambling for something to fill the silence with. But this is a tough tactic to employ because, of course, the temptation and pressure will therefore be on you to also fill the silence. However, if you can master the pause, you will be an excellent negotiator (see the quote at the end of this chapter).

3. **Paraphrase:** This is especially useful if you feel that the other person is not really listening to your side of things, and this happens a lot in negotiation. A lot of the time people are so pre-occupied with their side of the story and what they want, that they don't really listen to what you have to say. And we can establish if they're doing this by listening to how they begin their sentences. If they start sentences with 'Yes, but...' or 'But...' we know for a fact that they haven't really listened to our previous message (see also chapter 3: Personal Interactions). This means we should keep paraphrasing our main points until we're sure the other side gets our message. For example: "The best delivery date I can make is next Thursday." "I understand you need the items by next Tuesday, but my raw material suppliers have only just delivered to my manufacturing plant, which means that Thursday is the earliest." "What I can do is deliver some

of the items by Tuesday with the remainder coming on Thursday."

4. **Ask Questions:** Don't take things at face value all the time. Probe a bit more, especially if you notice a shift in body language, face touching or looking away from you as they speak. These are clues that the other side may be hiding some useful information. Get them to explain things further or clarify a particular point. What's more, if you feel that you're getting stuck in the negotiation, some of the best questions to ask are 'What if...' questions. These are hypothetical so there's no commitment from either side, just an exploration of what may be possible. In effect they put the situation back in the other side's territory, so he or she has to answer your suggestion and defend it. For example: "I appreciate you've set your heart on going to New Zealand for our honeymoon, but what if we go to Australia this year, because of the special airfares, and we go to New Zealand next year, or when we save enough money to have a really exciting time there?" Finally, you can also use leading question tags to make the other side feel as though they want something i.e. you lead them to the answer of your choosing. For example, "You don't want to work late in the office every day, do you?" Or "You want to close this deal as soon as possible, don't you?" With these types of questions, it's more difficult for the other side to answer any other way than 'Yes'. And then you have the advantage again.

5. **Ask for a Favour:** This is probably the most common influencing tactic that you hear in negotiations, but if

used judiciously it can produce excellent results. There is a risk though, which is if you ask for a favour, the other side can also do the same. And if they've conceded to you, they will expect you to also do the same. Further, you don't want to be labelled as the person who always asks for favours, so use this tactic thoughtfully and selectively.

6. **Emotional Disclosure:** When used wisely, this can have a significant effect on the negotiation, particularly when things are getting a bit heated. By voicing out how you feel, you release the tension that builds up and gets in the way of thinking clearly and creatively. This has the effect of disarming the other side, as most cultures are brought up with the thinking that a person should hide their emotions. However, in a negotiation it shows strength, and by surprising the other side with your openness, you will appear more assertive and confident.

7. **You have to do better than that:** When you get to the point where final offers are made, there's the temptation to give in and accept the good deal you have hopefully negotiated for. Don't. Instead, say to the other side the statement: "You'll have to do better than that". Or similar. I'm always astounded that when I use this phrase, people often give more away. You would think that after they've made their final offer and anchored to it, you would both see that nothing more can be gained by pushing further. But there is, and it works. I agree that sometimes in a negotiation you've pushed the other side to the point of exasperation and to push any further would lead to an

aggressive outburst, so use this tactic shrewdly. Nevertheless, use it as often as you can as it gets results.

To the astute reader you may be thinking that you've used all of these techniques at some time or another, and that's not surprising as these are well-known and the best techniques you can use. However, most people don't use them consciously as tactics; they use them at a subconscious level and usually just one only. What you would be wise to do is arm yourself with all of them and consciously use the one you think most appropriate at the time. Then, as the negotiation moves along, use a different one. The main point here is to use the tactics consciously. This will give you a huge advantage over anyone who hasn't previously considered how they're going to approach the negotiation.

Patience is a virtue so they say, and in negotiation this is certainly true. Wait: there's no need to be in any hurry to make the first offer or lay all your cards out on the table. Get to know the other side as much as you can, and if they are in a hurry, then let them make the first offers. If you are in a hurry, my advice is to pitch as high as possible and anchor to that point i.e. stick to it as much as you can. After all, there are many things outside price that can also be negotiated. For example, the time it takes for something to be done. Or payment terms - does everything have to be paid at once? Or quality: are there any variables here?

Then keep asking questions. Agree and disagree as you wish, but also keep probing for more information so you can be sure you've got the whole picture and explored all the variables. A particularly good question to ask is "How did you arrive at that figure/price/time/date?" And although it can be a bit irritating if you do it too much, you can always answer a question with a question. For example: "I know you can afford it. Why can't you accept this price?" "How do you know I can accept this price?" Or "Why can you only deliver on Fridays?" "Why is Friday such a problem?" And so on. It's nearly always possible to ask a question to gain more leverage, but again make sure you have an armoury of a variety of questions otherwise it will sound repetitious and insincere.

If the tables get turned and you find yourself defending your position or having to justify your statements, use benchmarks (such as market value) and previous settlements as the standards you are abiding by. This will make your arguments look fair and equitable. The more established benchmarks or examples you have to support your case, the more powerful your proposal will appear.

If you do find yourself under pressure, make sure you pause before you answer the questions the other side is throwing at you. For example, with the question "Why do you keep asking us to buy all the time?" there is a temptation to take a defensive stance before answering the question e.g. "We don't." Get rid of the negative reaction ("We don't") and use the pause to say the second part of the message i.e. what you really mean – "We want our customers to be aware of the special offers that come up from time to time."

Here's another example: "Why are your mortgages so expensive?" "They're not." (This is a typical reaction, which you want to get rid of before you mention the real answer which follows.) "In comparison with a number of other banks and building societies, our pricing is very competitive. And the quality of the support service we offer is excellent."

Pitfalls

There are also some pitfalls to watch out for. The most common of which involves 'price range'. Whenever you are thinking of making a substantial purchase, or sometimes at a job interview, you will be asked "What price/salary range are you looking at?" In reality, there's no such thing as a range in negotiation. The seller is only interested in the highest figure you mention and how much he or she can push you above that. Conversely the buyer is more focussed on the lower figure or how much less they have to pay. Try to avoid ranges by saying something like "Perhaps you could show me some of the choices I have?" and if they insist by asking you again for a range so they can show you something appropriate, you can counter by saying "Show me something in the middle of your range and we'll take it from there." Or, you can just tell them honestly why you prefer not to give them a range.

Another pitfall to watch out for is lying or bluffing. Once you get trapped in a lie it becomes harder and harder to escape. Certainly, there are times when you don't want to tell the whole story and can leave things out, but be very careful about telling a lie as they have a nasty habit of creeping up on you when you least expect them.

Also be wary when people ask you to negotiate over the phone or by email. It's far easier to say 'No' than if you are face-to-face with the person. Having said which, if the negotiation is not that important, then yes, go ahead if it saves time and money. However, the Golden Guideline is to always negotiate face-to-face when the negotiation is important, then you get a wealth of visual clues to assist you.

Something else to look out for is being drawn into an argument. The other side may deliberately try to provoke you into getting emotional, just to upset your train of thought. A fairly common provocation is to start the negotiation with a ridiculously high figure. Rather than get annoyed, ask them how they can justify such a figure and ask for supporting evidence. Listen to what words you use to try and keep them factual (high, justify, small, etc.) rather than emotional (ridiculous, no way, stupid, etc.).

Not so much a pitfall as a challenge is when the other side questions your authority, qualifications or status. This is often the case in Asia and especially when the other side is considerably older than you. If you feel the query is genuine and they want reassurance that you are a decision-maker, then avoid taking offence and answer politely. If you are not a decision-maker then you may be wasting their time and they will probably want to close the negotiation quickly and ask to speak with someone who is, which, when you think about it, is fair.

The End Bit

There are really only two things to remember at this point: don't give anything away as a parting gift to appear 'nice'; and don't go back and negotiate something that's already been agreed, unless the other side is prepared to re-look at all the variables again.

The number of times I've been in a negotiation and the other side offers me something for free at the end, just because they want to appear a good person is incredible. In my opinion this is probably the greatest mistake that a negotiator can make. Remind yourself that you've worked hard to get what you want, so don't give anything away without getting something in return. Otherwise, it makes the whole process a waste of time and undermines your credibility for the next time you meet the same person.

A tactic used by some negotiators is to ask for changes to the agreement just when you think they are prepared to close the deal. This can take the inexperienced negotiator off balance and result in them giving away items that had been previously negotiated and hard to get. The opposition will make the concessions they're asking for appear very small and no more than a parting gesture from you. My advice is to say it's not possible since it's something which has already been agreed. However, if they start insisting, then say that they must be prepared to re-negotiate other items in ***your*** favour too.

Finally, make sure there's some sort of written record of the agreement for both parties. This can be an email, memo, scrap of paper, a recording. It doesn't matter what it is, but just have something that you can refer to if necessary, as all our memories are fallible and open to misinterpretation at a later date.

'Never forget the power of silence, that massively disconcerting pause which goes on and on and may at last induce an opponent to babble and backtrack nervously.'

Lance Morrow

Summary

1. Always make your opening pitch as high as realistically possible.

2. Never give anything away for free, always trade for something in return.

3. Prepare, and then prepare. After this, prepare.

4. Create as many variables in your favour as possible.

5. Ask questions until you know there are no assumptions on either side.

6. Manage your EI and SI to give you more of an advantage.

7. Have the mindset that you'll enjoy the negotiation.

8. Read 'Hirst on Negotiation: winning hearts and minds'

12. Meetings

> **'Meetings are a symptom of bad organisation: the fewer meetings the better.'**
> *Peter F. Drucker*

If you work in a company where the boss likes to have lots of meetings (Zoom or face-to-face), or stuck on a social committee that always seems the need to convene, you are allowed to feel a little sorry for yourself. But it's not the end of the world: writing the minutes of the meeting is. That job has to be up there with cleaning the toilets with a toothbrush. And whatever you write will be wrong, unless you have an excellent boss or chairperson who allows you to tape the meeting so you have the reference points later. That and the boss understands you cannot be expected to write exactly the same way as he or she does.

I digress. Two things in life are inevitable: death and meetings. At this particular time of Covid 19, nearly all of them are taking place online; however, this is likely to change once things get back to normal. If meetings are successful, they can increase revenue, enhance relationships, and solve problems. Unfortunately, the majority of meetings waste time and resources because they are badly organised and poorly executed. This can lead to frustration, resentment and lost revenue, which can run into millions of dollars. Therefore, meetings should achieve their purpose in the minimum time necessary, leaving people more time to attend to things that they are actually paid to do, or want to do.

Have a look at the questions below to see how well you do in meetings: the higher the score, the better. Anything less than thirty and you'd be advised to read the rest of this chapter.

How Do You Measure Up?		*Not True – Very True*
1.	I prepare thoroughly for every meeting that I attend, no matter what my role.	1 2 3 4 5
2.	I know what I want to achieve before every meeting.	1 2 3 4 5
3.	I always look through the minutes of the last meeting beforehand.	1 2 3 4 5
4.	I confidently share my point of view at meetings.	1 2 3 4 5
5.	I demonstrate confident body language at meetings.	1 2 3 4 5
6.	I always wait for others to stop speaking before I begin.	1 2 3 4 5

7.	I am able to control the tone of my voice during meetings.	1 2 3 4 5
8.	I always research others' points of view beforehand.	1 2 3 4 5
9.	I give in when I know I'm wrong.	1 2 3 4 5
10.	I express myself well during meetings	1 2 3 4 5

The first question you should ask yourself is whether a meeting is really necessary or not. It is way more expensive than calling people on the phone. There's a problem, so you call someone. There's a bigger problem, so you call a meeting. However, if you consider the issues a little more carefully, you can usually arrive at a solution without having to steal other people's time. Because that's what meetings do.

I realise that most of you reading this may not yet be in a position to call meetings, and are merely told you have to attend one of your bosses'. Nevertheless, you still have a number of things you can try to make the best of the situation. But first, add up the number of meetings you attended last month and then multiply this by the average number of minutes (hours) you spent in them. This gives you a figure of how much of your time is spent in meetings: the figure is usually quite scary.

What goes wrong?

The biggest mistake people usually make is not having a proper agenda, yet many people who call meetings claim there is one. However, when you look closely, you'll see that it's usually no more than a list of items. That is not an agenda. An agenda consists of the list, yes, but it should also say what the proposal or purpose is for each of the items. Further, it should indicate what the expected outcome of the proposal is, and it should state how much time is expected to be spent on each item. Finally, it should be sent out so people have enough time to view it and reply with any ideas, reservations or comments, so the document can be revised, thus saving time when it comes to the real thing.

I wonder how many people take the trouble to do that. I also wonder if people ask for an agenda if one isn't initially given.

Another great sin of meetings is not having anyone to take the minutes and write them up at the end. Without a clear record of the main points and of who was going to do what, the meeting will be a waste of time. People forget at the best of times, and in a meeting with many items up for discussion, it's very easy to get lost. It is therefore crucial to have a record of what is expected from each participant and when it will be achieved by.

Another major crime of meetings is that everyone and their pet are invited. Time is a very valuable commodity, so consider if everyone is really necessary. Is anyone there just for the sake of it? Wouldn't it be simpler and more efficient if they just get a copy of the minutes? Do you steal people's time?

So, What Should Happen?

A good agenda is a great place to start, and it should fulfil the following:

- Remind participants
- Focus attention on the issues
- Encourage participants to plan
- Be the structure of the meeting
- Stimulate action

Although too many people use it as an excuse, it is possible to build an agenda for an unscheduled meeting right at the beginning. It should still focus attention, structure the meeting and stimulate action. Also remember to delegate someone to write the minutes or some form of written record before the meeting starts. To help you build the agenda, unscheduled or otherwise, you can use the following questions to help you assemble your thoughts:

- What's the objective or the purpose of the meeting?
- To achieve these objectives, what do you need to achieve in the meeting?

- Who do you need to be present? Are you sure they have to be there?
- What information do you need people to bring?
- Who's writing the meeting up?

Then again, the majority of people reading this are those that have to sit in meetings rather than chair them. But the person leading the meeting is crucial to your participation, and you have a responsibility to help them by making sure you abide by the following:

1. Turn up on time.

2. Look through the agenda, and if there isn't one, ask for one.

3. Prepare what you're going to say for your part, and consider what input you might like to add to the other items.

4. Listen attentively, even if the subject is not directly related to your expertise.

5. Don't be afraid to interrupt a speaker. But be careful when you do it. Interruptions are only effective if they are at the right time.

6. Look at all the people present when you speak, not just the chairperson.

7. Be polite when you disagree with something that's been said, and avoid threats.

8. Give other people a chance to speak; don't dominate.

9. Ask for clarification if you're not sure about something.

10. Keep focussed and avoid getting side-tracked by incidental issues.

11. Take notes if you think it will help you later. Don't rely solely on the minutes.

12. Try not to show your frustration. Keep your emotions in check.

Naturally, guidelines are easier to write about than they are to follow, and each manager has their own way of conducting meetings. But there is one thing that nearly always happens: they overrun. Meetings nearly always take longer than they were scheduled for. What can you do about it? Well, apart from keeping your part brief, and encouraging others to do the same, not a lot really. It's up to the Chair of the meeting to make sure the items are discussed in a timely manner.

Mistakes made in meetings can vary from people having a hidden agenda to a complete hijack of the proceedings. The following are some of the more common ones:

- Bringing up a point that has already been discussed in the same meeting
- An overuse of jargon, particularly when some of the people present will not understand what you mean.
- Using the meeting to complain without offering a potential solution.
- Looking disinterested when you don't think the point being made is important.

- Using the phrase 'same as last time' or 'same as before' at every meeting.

When it comes to taking decisions, there are basically two types: authority and consensus. The key strength of authority is that it saves time: it's quick. The chief drawback is that the person being delegated may not be the right person for the job, and motivation may not be as high as when there is everyone's agreement. Conversely, consensus can take a long time, and even then, complete agreement may still not be reached, which ultimately leads to compromise. However, you are more likely to get buy-in from the participants. Often the situation will determine the best route to take. For example, if you intend to take a majority vote on something, consensus is the way forward. On the other hand, if there is strong disagreement from a variety of parties which cannot be resolved, or the issue is simple and straightforward, then an authoritative instruction is better.

The Physical Layout

Although you may not have much choice in the matter, a quick note on the layout of the room warrants a mention. The best arrangement for consensus building is a round table with the chairs evenly spaced around it (fig.1). This way, no particular person is using the space to create authority advantage. Moreover, the shape of the table means that people are working together rather than opposing each other as in the square table.

(fig.2). If people at the meeting feel that they are opposite each other, with the table acting as a barrier between them, then it will be psychologically harder to reach an agreement.

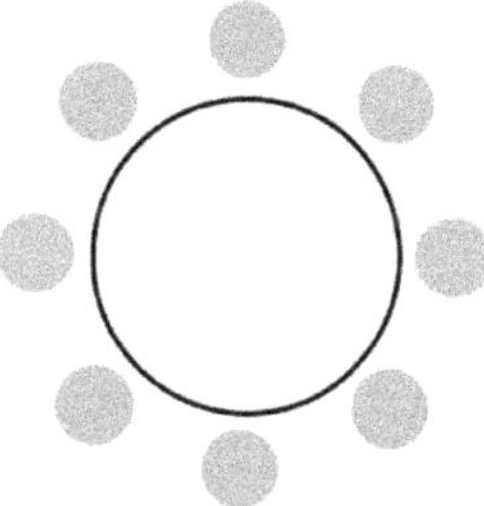

Figure 1

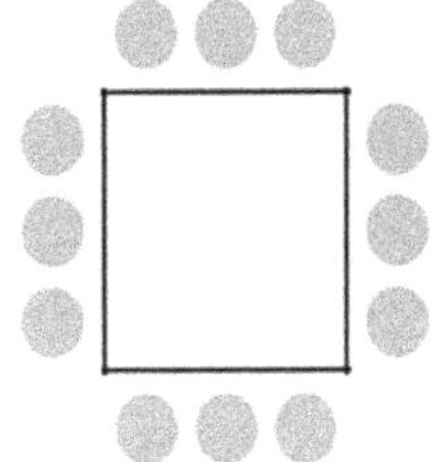

Figure 2

Another, perhaps more common configuration is the board meeting table as in figure 3 below.

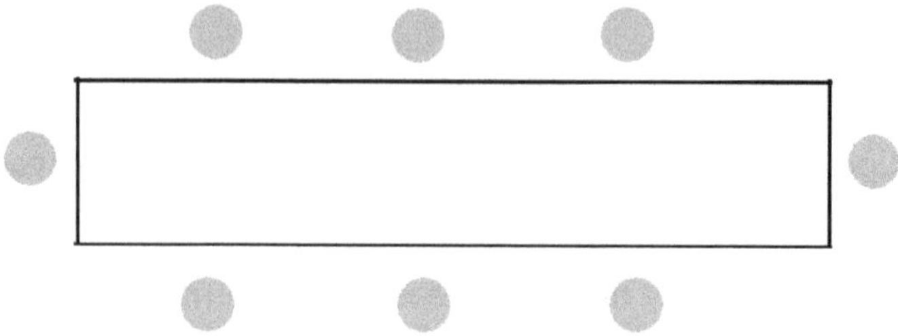

Figure 3

This arrangement tends to add more formality to meetings, which may be an advantage if that's what you're looking for. However, the boss will often sit at one of the ends and this makes it harder for him to control the proceedings. If he or she sits in the middle, the meeting may be easier to control, but it's still not ideal if you wish to build consensus.

Another common layout, particularly for meetings with a large number of people is the 'U' shape (fig.4).

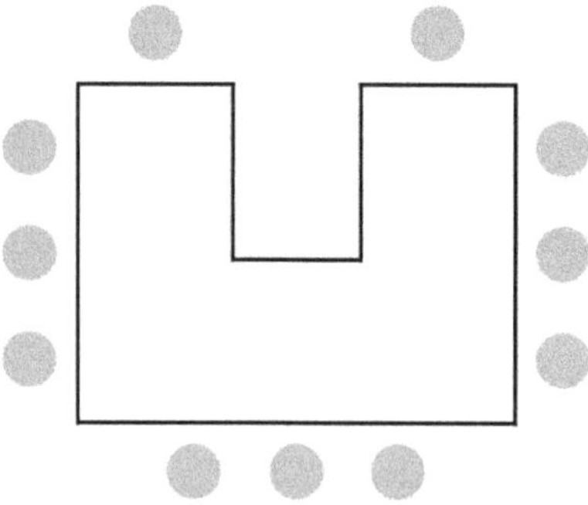

Figure 4

The main advantage of this is that everyone can see each other and they have a desk space. The disadvantage is that people can be physically far away from each other, which makes it harder to get buy-in from other members, or to get everyone's attention at the same time.

In summary, if you have a limited number of people, then I recommend using round or trapezoidal tables to encourage participation. However, if you are after control then the board meeting table is best. If you are not calling the meeting, then sit where you have the best chance of making your views heard by everyone, which is usually in the middle or next to the Chair of the meeting.

Online (Zoom/MS Teams) Conferencing

Online conferencing is preferable over phone conferencing as you get the luxury of seeing the expressions and other body language that is key to helping you form an opinion as to how they think about your ideas. Almost overnight, phone conferencing has disappeared. The rules are almost the same.

Before the Conference Begins

- The person calling the conference should ensure the following:
- An agenda that's been circulated.
- The equipment/pc/sound system has been checked.

- Rules for turn-taking and other aspects of the communication i.e. who will speak next, and who will take the minutes, have been established.

During

The person calling the meeting should first introduce everyone including those who are just listening in. Remember that the sound quality from microphones from in-built systems can be challenging at the best of times. Further, there may be some time lag due to internet connectivity. Not everyone needs to speak, but all should be invited to comment. One at a time, naturally. Dates should then be decided if there is to be a follow-up. The person who organised the meeting should also be the one who sums it up. As with all meetings, keep to the agenda timing.

After

The minutes or notes should then be distributed to all the people who were online and CCd to the people who had previously requested them.

Top Ten Zoom/MS Teams Conferencing Tips

- Familiarise yourself with your audio and mic settings.
- Let everyone know the agenda and follow it.
- Understand and use the software features e.g. background blur.

- Arrive slightly early in case there are connection problems.
- Wear appropriate clothing.
- Look at your camera (not people) when you speak.
- Interact and involve the others with an occasional question.
- Make sure you unlikely to be disturbed.
- Manage your gesturing and remember to smile.
- Technical difficulties happen. Be patient. Have a back-up plan.

THE WORST JOB OF ALL: Writing the Minutes

I'd literally do any other job in the office than have to write the minutes of meetings because it's such a thankless task. It will often seem that whatever you write and whatever style you write them in, you will have people complaining to you. However, they are a necessary evil as they should describe: -

- The date and time of the meeting
- Who was at the meeting.
- Who should have been there, but was not.
- What was discussed.
- What actions were agreed and why.
- Who should be responsible for implementing each action.
- The deadlines and timetable for completing each action.
- The items to be carried over to the next meeting.

If you have an informal club or society meeting, they will usually allow you to record the meeting. This gives you the opportunity to listen to it later and therefore spend the time in the meeting more profitably. And the same goes for a nice boss in a work-related meeting. However, for private and confidential, you may not be allowed to do so. In this case, you will have to either learn shorthand very quickly or become very efficient at note-taking. You can still use the agenda to help, of course. And I'd also recommend a clear layout with liberal use of sub-headings to help the writer (and the reader) group items together.

When you write the minutes of meetings, the modern way of business writing tends to go out the window. There is more use of the 'Passive Voice' and the 'Past Perfect' tense. Both are otherwise usually avoided. The key element is that everything you report goes back one grammar tense. It's this part of the writing that confuses most people. For example, if I report the question: "Do you speak English?" I have to put it in the past tense: 'He asked if she spoke English' (notice there's no question mark when I report the question). It becomes even more confusing when we report the answer "Yes, I do." When reported it becomes 'She said that she did.' Well, she still does and will do in the future, but we use the past tense because that's when the conversation took place. Confused? Yes, I understand, and while most companies have their own conventions of writing, here are some practical guidelines that you can use in just about any situation.

One tense back

A good knowledge of the grammar of reported speech is required when writing the minutes of a meeting.

Actual words: *"There can be no more unlicensed drivers allowed on the rally course this year."*

Minutes: The Chairman of the club said that there could be no more unlicensed drivers allowed on the rally course this year.

In reported speech

Will	becomes	would
Can	becomes	could
May	becomes	might
Must	becomes	had to
Shall	becomes	should/would
Is/Are	becomes	Was/Were
Was/Were	becomes	Had been
Have/Has +V3*	becomes	Had + V3*

***V3 refers to the past participle – the third part of the verb**

Reporting Sentences

"We have a deal."	becomes	(S/he said) we had a deal.
"We had a deal."	becomes	(S/he said) we had had a deal.
"I have made a deal."	becomes	(S/he said) s/he had made a deal.
"There was a deal."	becomes	(S/he said) that there had been a deal.
"There had been a deal, but it was no longer valid."	becomes	(S/he said) there had been a deal, but that it was no longer valid.
"There will be a deal next week."	becomes	(S/he said) there would be a deal next week.

Another area that minutes change from normal business writing is in the use of the 'Passive Voice'. There tends to be much more use of this in minutes as there is more focus on the action taking place than the person doing it. For example:

Spoken in the meeting *"We* ***will close*** *the shop over the Christmas period."*

Reported in the minutes Mr Plup said that the shop would be closed over Christmas.

The other main element of grammar that needs changing is pronouns such as 'me, you, him, her, it, us, them, we, they, I, he, and she'. For example

Spoken in the meeting *"We must receive your calculations before the end of the month."*

Reported in the minutes He stressed that they had to receive their calculations before the end of the month.

One key issue when writing minutes is that the spoken language used in a meeting is often quite informal, whereas the minutes of a meeting are expressed in a more formal, written style. This has an effect on more than just the grammar, for example your choice of vocabulary is likely to be more formal.

Spoken in the meeting: *"I'd like you to get in touch with Mr. Leaf as he's the person who's managing the project, and find out what his revised cost predictions are by this coming Thursday. His mobile number's on the project management team's list if you'd like to give him a bell."*

Reported in the minutes: The Chair asked the company secretary to contact Mr. Leaf to obtain the revised cost predictions by Thursday 20th June.

Although the main task of the writer is to report the facts of the meeting, it is also his or her responsibility to reflect what each speaker actually does with his or her words. There is a wide choice of reporting expressions to choose from. For example, the writer should indicate whether the speaker 'stated, mentioned, explained, told, informed, notified, or updated', etc.

It's a similar case with requests. For example, 'requested, enquired, wanted, asked for, or demanded', etc.

Spoken in the meeting: *"When will this project actually get started?"*

Reported in the minutes: Head Accounts asked when the project would get started.

Opinions, and agreeing or disagreeing with them, also have their own language changes. However, take note that the writer should report the facts and decisions as much as possible and be very wary of arguments and opinions. For example:

Spoken in the meeting: *"I think the annual dinner should be put on ice for the time being."*

Reported in the minutes: The Chair *felt/considered/thought* that the annual dinner should be postponed until a later date.

If there is agreement or disagreement with a proposal, the following can be substituted:

The management agreed (that.../with...) / accepted that…

The management did not agree (that.../with...) / disagreed with... / did not accept that... / found it unacceptable that…

Words and expressions of time is another area that changes, as the minutes are written later than when the actual meeting took place. For example:

Yesterday	**becomes**	the previous day / the day before
Today	**becomes**	that day
Next week	**becomes**	the following week
Next month	**becomes**	the following month
Two weeks ago	**becomes**	two weeks previously
Ten months ago	**becomes**	ten months previously

Spoken in the meeting: *"The project will be completed next week."*

Reported in the minutes: S/he said that the project would be completed the following week.

How can I improve my minutes writing?

This is the sixty-four, million-dollar question. The answer is actually very simple, free and not overly time consuming. And it can be fun. Go to the internet. There is a wealth of information, games, ideas and exercises on reported speech, which for most people is so much more interesting than working through a grammar book.

Click onto your favourite search engine and then type in 'Reported Speech Games' into your browser. You should then get lists and lists of English language schools. And many of them have online learning resources which you can access for free. Avoid the ones that ask you to register or request your email address as you run the risk of getting spammed. Once in the resource section, you should be able to select your level of difficulty. I recommend starting with something simple first, just until you get the hang of things. Then, after a while, move on to the more challenging stuff. A good site will not only have fun exercises, but will also let you know which you got right and which you got wrong, and, more importantly, why. It's such a fun way of learning, even for those who are not so tech-savvy.

'A collection of a hundred great brains makes one big fathead.'

Carl Jung

Summary

So much time is wasted in meetings, but still club committees and managers insist on having them, and then spend half their time chatting about items that are not even on the agenda (if there is one). So much more could be achieved if less unnecessary meetings were called. Nevertheless, at certain times it is important to have progress or decision-making meetings, and as a result of these, action should take place that moves the club or company forward. In my opinion, if no action takes place then it was a waste of time, and the information could have been sent by email. So, think carefully before you call a meeting, and when attending, be brief and knowledgeable.

13. Business Writing

'To find out your real opinion of someone, judge the impression you have when you first see a letter from them.'

Arthur Shopenhauer

Many books are written on this subject. The one I wrote is called 'Business Writing (3rd Edition Amazon): the evolution of writing with style and impact'. Rather than reprint large chunks of that book, I've decided to offer a series of model messages you can use as a basis for most, if not all of your written communication. Even if you don't fancy the idea of browsing through my book, I would also urge you to go to your nearest bookstore and at least have a look at some of the others which are available. Nearly all of them carry a wealth of information.

The Death of Letters.

Let's face facts: letters are a dying class of correspondence. Communication is mostly done electronically (Email, Zoom, Sms, Chatrooms, Facebook, Twitter, P2P programmes, Skype, etc.), and this trend will continue until the letter is finally dead.

However, business letters still exist and fall under five main categories:

1. **Sales**
2. **Enquiry & reply**
3. **Writing and replying to complaints**
4. **Collection**
5. **Refusals**

As most of these letters are still likely to be sent via email, I've either added an email version underneath any model letters given, or the answer is in the form of an email only. I've also added comments to take this into consideration at the end of each example.

1. Sales

Sales letters have changed considerably since the 90s and 2000s as most information from the seller is put online for anyone to access it. However, if the product is new or there is new information about it, you still have to let people know and get them to visit the site. However, most of these messages are sent via email informing people about the website or Facebook page more than the product itself, and the sales letter has been relegated to informing existing customers who are not contactable via an electronic medium. The previous notion that the letter would get people to go down to their local shops and buy the product, required careful crafting. Now though, the purpose is for the potential customer to look online for more information. They have therefore become more of a tease than a full-blown, informative communiqué.

Sales letters have also become more personal. Most people realise that 'Dear Valued Customer' is so clichéd that the message goes straight in the bin. It's almost mandatory to use the person's name you are addressing, and if that's not possible, then a more personal greeting such as 'Hi Bargain Hunters' is likely. These days it is also more probable to have the message (website) designed on an item, a card, or something else that is likely to attract the attention of the potential customer. Nevertheless, whatever the message is on, the key rules apply: **attract**, **connect** and **trigger action.**

To **attract** the reader, there will be considerable use of adjectives to create a vivid picture in the reader's mind of the product or service. Then, the **connect** part will have greater use of 'you' compared with other letters to make the message appear more reader-focussed. And finally, the **trigger action** part will feature the next step for the potential customer, and how easy the next step will be e.g. 'Just click on the link below and you'll be able to see the full range of our services to help you get more from your car.'

For example:

Dear Mr Ah Pek

I note from our records that it has been over a year since you last visited our store to purchase our special hair formula. This has come to our attention as you used to be one of our regular customers and it was our pleasure to serve you.

You always seemed very pleased with the success of 'Wondergro', and I am anxious that for some reason you have been dissatisfied with either our sales staff or our product. We are very concerned with maintaining an excellent relationship with our customers and therefore enclose a reply-paid envelope for your comments on how we can best meet your needs in the future. Instead, you may like to log on to www.wondergro.com where you will find a 'contact us' section to send us your comments.

Meanwhile, I'm enclosing our most recent catalogue of 'Wondergro' formulas including our latest 'SemiValu' product. We would also like to offer you a special 20% discount as a returning customer if you make a purchase within 30 days of the date of this letter.

I sincerely hope that this letter finds you in good health and we look forward to seeing you in our store in the near future.

Yours sincerely

The Email Version

Dear Mr. Ah Pek

I see from our records that it's been over a year since you last visited our store and we're wondering if all's well with you.

If you have any comments regarding our service, we'd love to hear from you. You can log on to www.wondergro.com where you can select the 'contact us' icon. Additionally, you can access our latest catalogue by following this link www.wondergro.com/catalogue

We would also like to offer you a special 20% discount as a returning customer if you make a purchase within 30 days of the date of this email. You can make your purchases online to save you the trouble of coming into town too.

All the best for now and please let us know if you'd like any more information about our products.

Regards
Siew Lien

Comment

First of all, it is much more likely that the message would be sent by email, and the difference (as you can see) is the use of more contractions and more personal language. It is as if the writer was speaking to the reader. In both the letter and the email, the opening paragraph gives the reason for writing and also attracts the reader and connects with them on a personal level. The second paragraph of both examples invites connection and participation from the reader. For the letter, it does this in two ways: by offering the chance to write back, or by accessing their website. For the email, it simply presents the web address. Given the nature of the product and the age range it's likely to attract, offering the postage-paid envelope for the written reply with the letter is a good idea. If the product was targeted at a younger audience, there would be no need for the self-addressed envelope as any reply is likely to be done online. The third paragraph of the letter up-sells (back-chains) their product i.e. offers the reader a product they may not have considered before, but may be interested in. The email version, however, simply gives information about the special offer to keep the message as brief as possible. This will hopefully trigger action. And finally, the last paragraph gives a polite close to the message. A final note on the letter is that although it's polite, it's almost bordering on grovelling. It's almost being too polite and the reader may wonder why. Another variation of the above could be to use the first sentence, then jump to the third paragraph, but perhaps begin it with 'Therefore,' (instead of 'Meanwhile'), followed by the close. You could also add an email address with the comment 'Please feel free to contact us at Enquiries @ ... if there's anything we can help you with.'

2. Enquiry & Reply

These days, most enquiries are also likely to be through email, which is what I'll give as examples here. And remember, emails should be exactly the way you would speak to the person.

The key elements for an enquiry are twofold: the message should be easy to understand and brief.

Email (Version 1)

Dear XY Services

I saw your website recently and I'm writing to enquire about your catering service for a wedding I'm planning next month for my cousin.

We expect approximately 200 guests and will be holding the service and the reception in the local Botanical Gardens.

I'm currently looking to source a suitable caterer for the event and am hoping you can provide me with more details regarding the services you provide. In particular, I'm keen to learn more about the following:

1. Pricing structure
2. Chairs/tables and other furniture you provide
3. PA system
4. Menus
5. Availability

I can be contacted at this email address, or you could phone me between 10am and 1pm, Monday to Thursday (012-3456 789).

Regards

Email (Version 2)

Hi Caterer Today

I'm planning my cousin's wedding for next month and expect apx 200 or so pax.

We'll be holding the function in the Botanical Gardens and are sourcing a suitable caterer.

Therefore, please let me know the following:

- Cost
- Any furniture you provide
- Mic and speakers
- Menus
- Availability

Please drop me a line at this address, or call between 10am and 1pm, Monday to Thursday (012-3456 789).

Thanks

Comment

The main difference between the two emails is one of tone; the first being slightly more formal than the second. It really depends on the people you are writing to. The key is whether the person reading it will have enough information to know how to reply with what the writer wants to read. When you're writing to people you have never met or don't know, it's always better to err on the side of politeness rather than friendliness. Therefore, I believe the first one to be more professional as you don't yet know the person you're writing to.

Golden Guideline

When you write any email, imagine the person is sitting in front of you. What you would say to them is exactly what you should write.

Reply

> Hi Calvin
>
> Thanks very much for your email requesting more information about our services.
>
> We pride ourselves on being very cost competitive, and I'm sure we can offer the best value for money for your cousin's wedding. Attached is our current price list.
>
> We'll be holding the function in the Botanical Gardens and are sourcing a suitable caterer.
>
> We also have a range of awnings and other furniture and PA systems we can include in the price. Additionally, we have 3 of our most popular menus on our website www.catertoday.co.uk although I'm assuming at this point that you would prefer to design your own.
>
> Perhaps we could meet up to discuss this either at our offices or at a place more convenient to you. My direct line is 883 777222 or you can call me on my mobile phone 017 7738883.
>
> Regards

Comment

The purpose of this reply is to build on the contact and try to arrange a face-to-face meeting. In most negotiations, a face-to-face meeting is better as it's more difficult to say 'No', and also the seller has more chance of convincing the buyer (see the chapters on body language and negotiation). The first paragraph acknowledges the initial enquiry. The second offers a key selling point and a theme for the writer to build on - and mentions the attachment. The third paragraph adds more of what the reader is likely to want and adds a link to their website. And finally, the last paragraph proposes a meeting.

In summary, the reply follows the format of acknowledge, satisfy, inform, then propose. By following this format, you are likely to build on any relationship and work towards a good deal for both sides.

3. Writing and Replying to Complaints

Writing Complaints

A good complaint letter is a work of art and should bring about a change in the service you receive, or compensation. The key thing about writing a complaint letter is that you can't change the past, so there's no point in dwelling in it. Of course, you will need to mention what the problem is, but keep it as brief as possible. They won't be interested in every detail, even if you'd like to point it out to them. Keep it brief and to the point. Secondly, focus on what you can change i.e. the future. It's always a good idea to mention what changes you think would benefit you and other customers. There's no need to be too specific about the compensation you think appropriate, but you can hint at what it would take to keep you as a customer. Thirdly, while there is a tendency to let all your anger and emotions flow, don't. All this does is make the other side feel less likely to help you and give you up as a lost cause. Keep your cool and concentrate on the facts. Next, avoid pointing fingers at the reader. Avoid using the term 'you' for two reasons: the first is that it may not be the reader's fault directly and they may just be a company representative. Secondly, no-one likes to have fingers pointed at them since it tends to make people defensive and less likely to do anything to help. In particular, avoid threats at all costs. Finally, use straightforward, sincere language. With complaints there is a tendency to let sarcasm come out, because it often feels good writing it and it's a way of letting out a little anger. The best thing to do is avoid it for the same reason that you should avoid expressing any emotions other than genuineness in this type of correspondence. In sum, the **Golden Guidelines** for writing a letter of complaint are as follows:

- **Keep it short and to the point.**
- **Concentrate on the future not the past.**
- **Keep your emotions in check.**
- **Avoid blaming individuals: do not threaten Be straightforward and sincere.**

Example: Complaint Letter/Email

Dear Sirs

Subject: Flight KLF 203, KLIA to London

I'm writing to inform you that the above delayed flight caused me to miss my connecting flight to Ireland, and I had to spend the evening in the airport hotel at my expense.

I asked the KLF representative whether they had made any arrangements for other passengers and they not only said 'No', but they advised us to wait in the airport if we couldn't afford the airport hotel. Although I was very angry at the time, I decided the best thing to do was let you know about this incident so you can avoid this happening again to any other customers.

Perhaps you will also consider reimbursing me for the cost of the hotel (a copy of the receipt is attached). I'm also happy to supply the name of the representative involved and other details if you require them.

I've always chosen your airline because of the good service and careful attention to detail, and was very surprised by this incident. I sincerely hope that your level of customer care is looked at carefully to avoid this happening in the future.

Comment

Initially you might think that the above example is too nice for a complaint letter and that it needs to be stronger, so the reader gets the feeling of how angry you are. However, that is exactly what the reader expects - an angry customer - and the reader simply turns off when reading it. The above example is a good complaint letter because there is no emotion, except hope (which is always a good thing), and it sticks to the facts of the case. It is likely to result in more than just a hotel refund.

Replying to Complaints

The key thing to remember when you receive a complaint letter or email is that it represents a last chance for you or your company to make things right and keep the customer. People who are really angry are more likely just to go to another service or product provider rather than write to you to complain about it. Email and WhatsApp do make things easier for the complainant to complain, but most of the time, ten minutes after the incident, the person has calmed down enough not to care about taking the time to write in. Therefore, the people who do should be treated as if they're holding out a last chance invitation - irrespective of the language they use.

There is also no need to go through each complaint the writer makes as all this does is remind the person why they complained in the first place. The best thing to do is avoid the past, because you can't change it, and concentrate on how things will be better in the future. In other words, create hope for the reader.

First, a good reply to a complaint is to thank the person for bringing this to your attention. While you may not feel like thanking a person who's angry at you, remember that they aren't: you are just the nearest person that they can off-load their anger on – they don't even know you, so don't take offence. Also try to reduce the number of trigger words that remind them of the anger. For example, substitute the emotive word 'complaint' for the word 'incident' or 'issue', or other more neutral words.

Then apologise for the situation. Never admit fault or you might find yourself in a court case, but you can apologise for the situation and empathise with the person. This shows the reader that you understand how they felt and that you would probably feel the same way too.

Third, you may need to explain the situation from your side. In fact, you or your company may not even be at fault, although this is the toughest part to write as the complainer is not looking for excuses, which may anger him or her even more. As with letters of complaint, avoid the word 'you', and use the passive voice if they are the ones at fault. The customer is not always right, but there's no profit to be gained from rubbing their noses in it i.e. telling them they were wrong.

Fourth, you might like to offer some sort of compensation. Unfortunately, many times people will ask for a ridiculous amount of compensation for really trivial complaints, but each one has to be dealt with on its merits. For example, asking for a month's free Travel Card when the ticket seller was a bit rude is not appropriate. If you're generous you might like to offer a free lounge pass and an apology, but the compensation should be commensurate with the grievance. With the example above, you may like to reimburse the cost of the hotel and perhaps something extra, although if you do this for one customer you will be expected to do it for all. Be cautious with the amount of compensation you give. **Finally**, and this is the key part, reassure the reader that things will be better in the future. Finish on the positive note of hope. In sum, the **Golden Guidelines** for replying to a letter of complaint are as follows:

1. **Thank the person for writing**
2. **Apologise for the situation**
3. **Explain – the why**
4. **Reassure and create hope**
5. **Offer compensation or action (if deserved)**

Below are two examples of replies to complaints. The first is one that buys more time for you to look into the situation. The second follows the guidelines above. The former covers Guidelines 1, 2 and 5 only and is often used when the letter is written badly, angrily or when you genuinely need to find out more about why the situations occurred. The second is a full letter highlighting all five Guidelines.

Example: reply to a complaint email 1

Dear Ms Noh Chan Su

Thank you for your email of 4 Feb 2019 informing us of your recent unpleasant experiences with a member of our staff. Please accept our sincere apologies for this.

We are currently looking into this matter and we would very much appreciate it if you could allow us a little time to investigate further. One of our senior managers from our Customer Relations Dept. will reply to you directly as soon as they have completed their investigations.

Once again, we apologise for any inconvenience caused and we thank you for your patience. *

Should you have any further questions at this time, please contact our Customer Relationship Executives on 1800 888 333.

Yours sincerely

* You may not feel that you need to offer a second apology at this stage, particularly if you think that it's not your company's fault. In this case you can simply leave this sentence out.

Example: reply to a complaint email 1

Dear Luk Ee Mann

Thank you for taking the time and trouble to complete a Passenger Feedback Form on flight KLF 203 and your email of 4 January 2019.

I am concerned to learn of the behaviour displayed towards you by a member of our ground staff. Please accept our apologies for this and may I assure you that rudeness from staff members is not tolerated and we take a serious view of such incidences.

Once again, I apologise that we did not live up to your expectations on this occasion. The Divisional Senior Vice President has been informed of this incident and will take steps to ensure that this does not happen again.

As a gesture of goodwill, we would be pleased to reimburse your hotel room cost upon receiving the receipt. I have also taken the liberty of crediting your frequent flyer account with 15,000 miles towards your next flight or upgrade.

Regards

4. Collection & Debt Recovery

This is always a tough one to write, and this is one of those rare occasions where the message is more likely to be in letter form than email. Usually, debt recovery comes in the form of a series of letters: the first reminds the person or company that they are behind with payment; the second becomes a strong reminder with the possibility of adding a specific time frame, beyond which there will be serious consequences; and the third or subsequent letter(s) lets them know what will happen if they do not pay. This last letter becomes more direct and accusatory. However, as with the complaint letter (or any message for that matter), never threaten the reader – more will be mentioned on this in the comment at the end of the examples. Nevertheless, there are ways to send a strong message without direct threats as we shall see in the three examples below.

Example: 1st letter - mild reminder

Dear Mr Zakar

Invoice # 456/Jan/21

It has come to our attention that the above invoice (copy attached) has been outstanding for three weeks.

As this has been a busy holiday period, I expect that this has just slipped your mind, particularly as your payment has always been prompt on previous occasions. Therefore, we would be grateful if you could make payment as soon as possible.

Yours sincerely

Example: 2nd letter - strong reminder

Dear Mr Zakar

Invoice # 456/Jan/21 and our letter of 4/Feb/21

According to our records the above invoice remains unpaid.

We wrote to you on 4th February 2011 to notify you of this, but we have yet to receive any reply from you.

Please settle the above account within the next 10 working days from the date of this letter to avoid any further action being taken.

Yours sincerely

Example: 3rd letter – final reminder

Dear Mr Zakar

Invoice # 456/Jan/21 and our letters of 4/Feb/21 and 21/2/21

Please note that despite our previous reminders (4 & 21 Feb 2011) we have still not heard from you, nor received any payment.

Therefore, you leave us with no other choice but to seek legal advice to recover the amount owed. This can be avoided only if you pay the full amount within 5 working days from the date of this letter.

Naturally we are hoping that this matter can be settled amicably and soon, and urge you to send payment today.

Yours sincerely

Comment

Hopefully you can see a progression in the letters from pleasant to unpleasant. This first letter even offers an excuse for the non-payment – the busy holiday period. The words chosen are positive and the tone is generally friendly. There is

no accusation at this stage, and the letter acknowledges that the payment may even be in the post.
In the second letter the tone hardens and the sentences are shorter and sharper, in fact each sentence is a separate paragraph, adding to its directness. Still there are no threats, but it gives an indication that something will happen if payment is not made, and it gives a clear time frame within which the payment must be made.

The third and final letter opens with reference to the previous attempts to contact the person and let them know that this has been ongoing, in the unlikely event that the previous letters were lost in the post. Then the main paragraph clearly states what will happen if payment is still not made. However, it is worded in a way to try and encourage the reader to make the payment. In particular it avoids phrases such as 'If you don't... we will (take legal action)'. As soon as you use this type of construction, you will be accused of threatening the reader which could add to a protracted legal battle to recover any losses. Additionally, when you use '...we will...' you have to be very sure that you will carry out your promise. I have known situations where companies have used '...we will take legal action' but in the end they didn't. This is either because it's too costly to do so, and the rewards are just not worth it, or that the legal department feels that the other party must be given further warnings before any action can be taken. In both cases, when you fail to carry out your threat, the reader is likely to then consider all future threats empty and therefore ignore them.

The way the threat has been avoided is by using the phrases '... you leave us with no other *choice/option* but to *seek/consider...*' This avoids saying they will, but 'seek/consider' sends a very strong message that protects the writer just in case management decide not to proceed with legal action. The rest of the paragraph then gives another chance for the reader to avoid this action. And the final paragraph extends a peace offering by phrasing the sentence in a friendly tone that uses the friendly word 'amicable' and 'urge'.

It is true that some companies may feel that this is still not strong enough and I have even heard managers say that they never get paid unless they threaten their readers. However, this is risky as the reader can also claim undue duress and file a court case against the writer. Further, most people react defensively when threatened which makes collecting payment more difficult, and even worse, it completely ruins any relationship you may have had with the reader.

5. Refusals

These are also quite difficult messages to write and can be in the form of letters or emails, the latter being much more likely.

The key thing about refusals is that the writer needs to be very sensitive to how the reader is likely to respond to the message. You may wish to say 'No' today, but you never know when you might want to say 'Yes' in the future, so always be considerate.

Example 1: refusing a payment extension request

Dear Ma Gi Mee

Insurance Policy xyz123

Thank you for your letter of 1 February 2020 requesting an extension of the payment date for the above insurance policy.

I regret to inform you that we are unable to extend the deadline for payment as it is now 2 weeks overdue.

To continue enjoying your current insurance coverage, I would be very grateful if you could make payment within 7 working days from the date of this letter.

I look forward to hearing from you, and please contact me at the above phone number if I can be of any further service.

Yours sincerely

Comment

In this example, the writer politely refuses the request and gives the reason for doing so. Then they create benefit by highlighting the advantage of keeping the insurance coverage. They could have used 'If you don't, then we will...' phrasing, but this would make the reader feel threatened and less likely to pay. Creating benefit is very important when you want something from the reader (or listener). And while it may be obvious to you, the reader or listener may need it highlighted. For example - spoken communication - instead of "Please fill out this form for us to process your application.", it's much better to say "To speed up your application, please fill out this form for us." The latter creates benefit for the listener. You can easily apply this to writing too. Instead of 'send payment within 7 working days', prefer 'To continue enjoying your current insurance coverage (creating benefit), please make payment...'

Another example of creating benefit in writing is in the example below, which is a reply refusing the request of a fee waiver on the use of a credit card.

Example 2: refusing a fee waiver request

```
Dear …

Thank you for your letter of 16 March 2020
regarding the annual fee waiver.

I am sorry (or 'I very much regret') to inform you
that we are unable to waive the fee of RM 100.00 (on
this occasion), which was charged in your February
2020 statement.

However, I would like to mention (advise you) that
with sufficient reward points, you may waive the
annual fee either in full or partially as follows:
```

For Steele Card

Reward Points Required	**Annual Fee Charged**
40,000	**RM 100**

To redeem the annual fee please contact our Blue Ocean Phone Bankers at 03 888 0000, who will be happy to assist you with this transaction.

Thank you for your understanding regarding this matter.

Yours sincerely

Comment

In this example, the writer politely refuses without explanation, but then the reader is probably aware that it is part of the terms and conditions of using the card. I've added brackets after some of the expressions as alternative choices to use. The created benefit is the explanation that the reader can use their accumulated points (from purchases) to offset the annual fee. This leaves the reader with the 'hope' factor, and is likely to leave them feeling okay about the refusal, or at least a resigned acceptance.

Things to remember when writing emails

The first thing to remember is to **check the address** before pressing 'send'. On a number of occasions, I've received emails that have subsequently been recalled, but then the damage has already been done. While checking the address, see if you really need to CC everyone on the list. Whenever you CC the message to people, you are stealing their time, so make sure that they really need to see the message. Yes, I realise that it's far easier just to click the 'reply to all' icon, and deleting some of the names takes you time, but it's a miniscule amount of time and people will thank you for taking the trouble.

Also check your subject heading. I notice that people who want to send you an email, will search through previous correspondence and simply press the reply button without changing the subject heading. Even more annoyingly they leave all the previous messages underneath without deleting them. It's fine when you wish to refer to previous correspondence, but when the new email is on a completely different subject it can be annoying. So, **check the subject heading** and **delete any previous irrelevant messages**.

Another useful tip is to **use numbered points** wherever appropriate. This gives the reader a reference point should they need to refer back to anything without having to repeat the main message again. Also, **read all your emails before you reply to any of them** since you may find that some are interrelated. And **wait before replying to any rude emails**. It's very tempting to respond immediately to nasty emails, but as I mentioned in the chapter on EI and SI, you will regret later what you write.

Finally, set your grammar and spell check to auto. They should be active whenever you write. They are not fool proof, so make sure you **read aloud before you press 'send** just to make sure.

Also recognise that most hand-held devices (mobile phones) use different operating systems from desk and laptops, so if you have any charts or graphs, it's always a good idea to put them as Word or PDF attachments. This way, the text will be easier to read and not broken by the addition of any graphics.

Things *not to do* when writing emails

- Don't use 'Smileys', unless it's a personal email.
- Don't use SMS abbreviations in emails, unless it's a personal email.
- Don't use caps lock (DON'T SHOUT), unless it's a personal email.
- Don't use excessive punctuation !!!???, unless it's a personal email.

Golden Guidelines for Emails

The following are a series of questions you really should ask yourself before you press the 'send' button. They pretty much cover all the information mentioned before, but are written here as guidelines for you to follow.

1. **Would you be comfortable saying this to the person's face?** It is easier to be blunter or even rude to a person through emails, so this is a great question to ask yourself to make sure that the tone of the message is right and you are not being impolite. Remember, emails should be written exactly the way you would speak to the person

2. **Would you be OK if the message was put on the company notice board?** This question reminds you that once you press the 'send' button, you have no control of where your email ends up. Too often people write something they shouldn't because they think it will reach the intended recipient and no other, but this is a very dangerous assumption. Even if you delete your in-box, out-box and so on, there's still a way to retrieve these messages, so be careful as to what you put out.

3. **Do I have permission to send this information?** This question is designed to remind you to think about the content of your message before you send. Are you revealing something P & C that in the wrong hands could do the company (or your image) damage? An

email is a legally binding business tool that can be used in a court of law, so if in doubt, remember Golden Guideline number 2.

What about Memos?

Memos are also a dying class of correspondence, but perhaps not quite as much as letters. The best advice I can suggest for memos is similar to the information I put in 'Business Writing: the evolution of writing with style & impact' (see below).

To:
From:
Date:
Subject: Structure and Style Guide for Memos

The following is a guide to the structure and style of writing memos as requested in your email of 28 Sept 2020. *

** Some writers feel that this first line is redundant and therefore unnecessary as it merely repeats the title*

Firstly, the subject heading should be brief. It may even be ungrammatical providing it clearly and concisely tells the reader what they are about to read. It is usually in bold and only two blank lines away from the main message.

How do you begin?

Your first sentence may contain a reference to the request or previous communication between the parties involved. However, the key point here is to get to the main message quickly, which is why we should avoid first lines such as 'Refer to the above' or 'With reference to the above…' (see also the footnote). You will also notice that I have dispensed with any greeting or salutation as they are unnecessary. A memo is much less personal than a letter and is usually addressed to a job title rather than an individual. It may also be read by more than one person in the office, making it more factual and less personal in nature.

Formatting?

If the memo is in the form of a report, consider using subheadings for various sections or paragraphs - particularly if the sections are quite lengthy. You should also consider putting these as the type of questions that the reader is likely to ask. You should also consider bullet points, especially if you have a list of items you wish to mention. For example, the following questions are very important when writing memo reports to create a logical flow:

- What's led to the current situation>
- What evidence do you have?
- What's the problem - can it be measured?
- What are the causes and effects (human, financial, etc.)?
- What are the possible solutions - and effects?
- Which do you recommend?

Conversely, if you are writing a more persuasive memo, you should consider putting the recommendations first and the rationale afterwards (logically).

How do you end

You will notice that there is no ending (as there is in a letter) because, like the salutation, it is unnecessary. The ending for most memo reports, and memos in general, is to lead a call for action - even if that action is merely filing the document for later reference. You should therefore consider ending your memos in a similar way to this one, or say what you'd like to happen and the date you'd like it to happen by. This can be in the form of a request to your boss, or a directive to your subordinates.

David Hirst *

* *You should put your name or initials here to clearly indicate that this is the end.*

And Finally, Grammar

English grammar is not easy and nearly everyone could benefit from brushing up their skills. It's not nearly as difficult as you may think. At this point I need to refer back to the chapter on meetings and, in particular, writing the minutes of meetings. There I described how you can easily improve your writing skill by going to the internet and playing some of the online games that most of the English language schools put out on their websites. It's fun, free, and these games can really help you. Naturally some sites are better than others, but half the fun is trying to locate a site you like the best. Then it's really just a matter of developing the habit of checking these sites out every now and again to brush up your grammar skills. Have fun.

'Think like a wise man, but communicate in the language of the people.'

William Butler Yeats

Summary

You must be wary when using model letters or emails for direction. They are excellent if you look at the way they're constructed, but dangerous if just copied. They best serve as guidance and are particularly good at helping you formulate your ideas about how to approach the message, but the words must be yours. This way, the message will come across as genuine and meaningful. It's all anyone could ask for.

14. Job Applications

'The closest a person ever comes to perfection is when he fills out a job application form.'
Stanley Randall

You've heard about the ideal job vacancy on a website, and they ask you to send in your resume. After an age of deciding what to leave in and what to leave out, and how to organise your qualifications and work experience, you sit down to write the covering letter. You know it should be brief, but another age passes before you write a letter that somehow just doesn't represent you well. There is so much you want to put down, but the right words are just inaccessible. When a sentence does seem near the mark, it turns out to be so long that it is impossible to read in one breath. In the end you resign yourself to using tired, archaic and semi-condescending phrases such as '...your esteemed organisation'. If any of this sounds familiar then this chapter is for you.

Or, you have heard about the ideal job vacancy on a website; you phone up and they ask you to attend an interview. This is important to you. You know this because you are especially nervous, and despite all your genuine beliefs that you would be perfect for the post, your mind is a confused jumble of fragmented advice. Your hands sweat and your heart palpitates.

In your mind, your words race like an F1 car and squeak when you try to say them. To make matters worse you know the interviewers can see the nervousness in your body language as clearly as they would a neon light on your forehead advertising the fact. If any of this sounds familiar then this chapter is especially for you.

The three main stages of job applications:

- Writing a professional Résumé
- Writing an effective covering letter
- Being successful in an interview

Writing a Professional Resume

Résumés, Curriculum Vitae, and covering letters are not written in order to secure a job.

Résumés, Curriculum Vitae, and covering letters are not written in order to secure a job. They are, in fact, to try and secure a job interview. They should therefore contain information to interest the reader(s), but not answer every possible question they might wish to ask you.

Nevertheless, as your application may be sitting in a pile with hundreds of others, what can you do to make yours get noticed - in a positive way? The answer lies in two areas: what you write and the style you write it in.

A growing number of companies are moving away from the traditional approach of requesting C.V.s and have their own

standard form for you to fill in. However, there will still be sections where they ask you to write your own version of why you should get the job. Therefore, much of the following will still apply. Furthermore, writing a good C.V. will put you in a better position for completing online forms, as you will have already thought about the questions which they are likely to ask.

Since the C.V. or Résumé usually forms the basis for the covering letter, it is typically written first. It should therefore be tailored to contain all the details relevant to the post you are applying for. This helps avoid the appearance of a standard and possibly tired- looking document that has no focus. If possible, it should fit onto one or two screen pages (maximum three for extensive experience), although this should not be at the sacrifice of layout quality and the use of white space to highlight the different parts.

There are normally 6 information sections:

1. Personal details
2. Education background
3. Qualifications
4. Employment History
5. Interests/areas of specialty
6. References

For example:

CURRICULUM VITAE: (Name...)

Date of Birth

Marital Status

Nationality

Current Address

Contact

Tertiary Education

Other Qualifications

Professional Development Courses

Chrono;ogy of Work-related Experience

References (or References on request)

Analysis

In this example, I've used the words 'Curriculum Vitae', although you could easily use 'Résumé' instead. I've used capital letters for the words, but title case i.e. just capitalising the first letter of each word would also be possible. Sometimes potential employers ask for a recent photo, but I hesitate when this is asked because some unscrupulous employers may judge your application based on how you look, so if you *have* to send one, then make it as flattering yet professional as possible.

Then comes the basic information. If nationality is obvious, there is no need to put it. And you may like to leave out marital status, unless you think it's an advantage to show that you're a family person; or if you're single, and therefore have no ties to keep you from extensive travel. 'Current Address' and 'Contact' could be combined into the former, but make sure that your email addresses are on a separate line to make them more easily accessible. Also, be careful what email address you give. If your only address is girlhunter@hotmail.com (as I actually saw once), then get a new one. Use something that is not going to offend or something neutral.

The next major section is where you put your qualifications. It is not necessary to put anything more than your degrees and post graduate diplomas here if you have them. However, with only one degree, then you would be wise to add your college or secondary schooling and the qualifications you took there. If you don't have a degree, then just put your secondary school and/or college and the qualifications.

The next section, 'Other Qualifications', is where you would put any language, IT, or any other skills or certificates. Or any other certificates or diplomas you obtained outside of schools, colleges and universities. If you don't have any of these then leave this section out, or better still, go out and get some.

You could also combine this with the next section which is 'Professional Development Courses'. These are courses that your current (or previous) employer will have trained you in. They could range from special software related workshops to health and safety to specialist machinery and so on. These are the courses that you needed to enable you to be more efficient in your current job, and do not necessarily offer you a certificate or diploma for having attended them. The key thing to remember is that although it may seem small to you now, it shows that you've taken the trouble to improve yourself. However, be selective and add only those things related to work. You do not need to let your potential employer know that you are a 'dog licence holder' or a 'member of the church choir' like I have seen on some applications.

Now you put in your work experience. For some this could be the largest section, although if you have had only one employer, you would expand on your roles and responsibilities. If you have held a number of positions in various companies, you would put down the key responsibilities and use this as a tease to get you the interview, where you could expound on them. If you have a number of jobs to put down, only give detail about the last post, otherwise the application will run into several pages and this will turn off the person reading it. After all, you're really only as good as your last job allowed you to be.

The following section is either 'areas of specialty' or 'interests' – especially if the sports you play indicate you are a team player. Generally, if you've had a varied work history or have been in a post where you've developed certain skills, this is the time to put them in. You could also use this section to highlight your main roles and responsibilities in your current or last job. For example, Business Development, Academic Management, Operational Management, Financial Management, etc. You can find much of this in your current job description. If you have little to put here, then you might like to change it to an 'Interests' section and put the activities you do to show you get along well with other people.

Unless you have any publications to your name, even if it's just in the company newsletter, you would then get to the references. Please let the people concerned know that you're putting their name(s) as your referee(s), and above all ask them if they're okay with this, just in case the company suddenly calls them up. Also, select your referees wisely i.e. one from your present employer, perhaps one from your previous employer or one from an academic, and one from a more general background. If you select two or even three from your present employer, then try to make sure that they come from different departments, or different offices. And most importantly, make sure that they are likely to say good things about you. Another possibility is just to write 'References on request', to let the reviewers know that you'd rather keep it quiet that you're applying for other jobs.

Writing an Effective Covering Letter

Although most job applications have gone electronic, you may still find yourself writing a covering letter which you can then upload with the rest of your application. You may also have to upload a C.V. as well, although many companies have their own format where you just fill in the missing information.

The covering letter is essentially a sales document with the sole purpose of getting you through to the next stage i.e. an interview. It is almost like a package of information to tease the reader into taking notice of you. It should contain expanded information related to the C.V. and not much more. It should also be as short as possible, as a concise message works best. The person going through the applications may have already looked at over a hundred other applications before even getting to yours, so keep to the point. You or the interviewer can expound on any points in the interview. The tone of the letter should be friendly, but neither too informal nor formal: a neutral style.

Above all, avoid complaining about your current job.

When it comes to adding 'made-up' information: don't. Lies will catch up with you in the interview. So, while I suggest that you can be economical with the truth, especially when it comes to a lack of experience or qualifications, emphasise the positive elements you **can** bring, but never tell an outright lie. Above all, avoid complaining about your current job.

Why a covering letter?

The covering letter sells: it should be clear and concise, and have an attractive layout. It should be like the foundations of a building. This will allow the interviewer to find out all the details through questioning. And always be prepared to answer details of whatever you put in the covering letter.

Length: the covering letter should be kept to one side of A4 paper. If this is difficult, because of the nature of your profession, then two sides at an absolute most.

Font: the same font should be retained throughout (Times New Roman & Century Schoolbook are the most popular).

Layout: the layout should be clear and attractive with good use of paragraphing. To highlight items, use bold or underline, but not both. Space is particularly effective.

Formality: it should be friendly but not too familiar. Over-formality will kill the reader's interest.

Rationale: include why you are interested in the post, but not at the expense of writing something negative about your existing job.

Use Positive Language: compare the following:
"I do not think that my existing job challenges me enough."

"I am looking for a post that will offer me a more challenging role."

Repetition: try to avoid repeating the same words in the letter: it looks clumsy. If you use 'I' a lot, then change the structure to vary its position in the sentence.

Active Voice: try and write in the active voice.

Editing: always wait a short while before sending the email. This gives you time (to clear your mind) before proofreading to check the accuracy and clarity of the message.

Making a Start

There are two schools of thought: the first is to start with why you are writing, but then that's what most of the other covering letters will do as well. The second is to vary the opening sentence slightly to make a difference. Compare the following:

Traditional

I am writing to apply for the above post as advertised in the Star of 23 February 2021.

Or

I'm writing to apply for the post of XYZ as advertised online on 23 Feb 21.

Or

I would like to apply for the above post as advertised in the vacancies section on your website.

Alternative

As I have been involved in conservation for some time, I am answering your advertisement in your website for the post of Fundraising Executive.

Or

Being an avid naturalist and conservationist, the position of Fundraising Executive as advertised on your website has a special appeal to me.

NB. In these cases you would put the job title in the subject heading.

You can see that the alternative versions grab your attention more because they're different, but in a positive way. And you will want your letter to stand out from the rest in a positive way, therefore being slightly different can become an advantage. For example:

Dear Mr Chin Chai

WWF Fundraising Executive Post

As an avid naturalist and conservationist, the position of Fundraising Executive as advertised on your website has a special appeal to me.

From my attached C.V., I have had nearly seven years' experience working in conservation. This has offered me several opportunities to work independently, particularly in the marketing and promotion of various events. The most recent sponsorship deal I negotiated involved coordinating overseas and local NGOs for the 'Wet Watch' campaign to create awareness of Malaysia's wetlands. The event brought in RM500k for ongoing projects.

Although I thoroughly enjoy my field of work, the NGO I am with is relatively small which means I have to look elsewhere for the challenges, exposure and greater responsibility that I would like. This is why I feel that my career would now benefit from a change.

I have informed my employers of this application and they will be happy to provide a reference upon request. My contract currently requires me to give two-months' notice although my employers have indicated that there may be some flexibility with this.

I would very much welcome the opportunity of an interview at a time convenient to you, and look forward to hearing from you in the near future.

Yours sincerely

Analysis

Following on from our discussion of the first paragraph above, the second paragraph makes reference to the enclosed/attached Résumé, and something about your current post. It mentions a bit about what you have learned from the current scope of work too. For every feature there should also be a benefit.

The third paragraph supports the above information and leads to the future i.e. what you are looking forward to doing.

Welcome an interview; be optimistic about the future, and finish on a positive note

The fourth paragraph contains any additional information you would like to include with regard to your references, your interests (if relevant), the amount of notice you have to give, or whether you wish to ask them not to contact your existing employer at this time. Your ending should indicate 'where would you like to go from here'. Welcome an interview; be optimistic about the future, and finish on a positive note.

There are few fixed rules, and you may find that altering the order of the above can add spice and interest to your application. However, the one thing to always avoid is repeating the information contained in the Résumé. The Résumé is there for them to see, so the covering letter should expound on that information, not just repeat it. In other words, take a fact from the C.V. / Résumé and then answer a 'Why' or a 'How' question.

For example, 'Why has this helped you achieve what you have', or 'how will this experience benefit the future company.'

The Interview

Although all the previous chapters will help you prepare for your interview, there are one or two extra things that are worth emphasising here.

The interviewee should:

- Study all the available information
- Dress well and appropriately
- Prepare to answer questions on all the information given
- Smile a lot (but not like a simpleton)
- Appear helpful and friendly
- Answer questions honestly – if you have to bend the truth, base it on fact
- Try to find commonality with the interviewer
- Have prepared some genuine questions for the interviewer
- Make the interviewer feel that the meeting went well
- Thank them for the opportunity of an interview

Recruiting is an expensive part of running a company. Therefore, getting the right person for the job is essential. Basically, organisations initially look for two things: Talent and Fit.

The successful person is the one who is put into the position where the natural talent can be used best.

A talent is a natural ability and not necessarily acquired through effort. Everyone has talent of some sort, and the successful person is the one who is put into the position where the natural talent can be used best. It is also important that the potential employee fits into the existing team if there is one.

In addition, interviewers look for a number of other things, and the following table outlines one example of the type of information the interviewer will want to find out more about.

Criteria for the Job	Exceeds	Meets	Does not meet	Experience & Skills
Personal Motivation: Takes initiative to learn and develop on the job as well as outside of work.				
Problem Solving - Cognitive Skills: Demonstrates the ability to analyse and solve problems.				
Administrative Skills: Displays a general knowledge of how to				

develop plans, organise work and manage time.				
Leadership Skills: Shows ability to guide others towards organisational goals and is accountable for the performance of department or team.				
Functional/Technical Knowledge: Has achieved a satisfactory level of technical skills/knowledge in job related areas and keeps abreast of current developments in areas of expertise.				
Special Abilities: Words? Numbers? Mechanical? Spatial? Creative?				
Mental and Emotional Attributes: EQ & SQ				

Analysis

Before they start filling out the items in the above table, the first thing that the interviewer will look at is your physical appearance. Then, having gone through your C.V. and covering letter, they'll have a basic idea about your education, skills, interests, and can probably hazard a good guess at your domestic life. After this, they'll ask questions to extract information related directly to the characteristics of the job. Most certainly, they will not ask a closed question such as 'Do you take initiative?', but they are more likely to ask something like 'Can you give us an example of when you've taken initiative and what the result was?' In fact, this type of question is likely throughout, so it's a good idea to prepare for it.

For the second part – problem solving – the question above is phrased along the lines of 'What problems have you overcome and how has this affected your effectiveness in the workplace?' Essentially, they're looking at how well your problem-solving skills have been developed through the course of your current employment. Similarly, administrative skill questions could arise in the form of 'What time management skills do you apply?', or 'Which IT programmes are you most effective with and how have you used them in the past?' They might also ask about your creative abilities and about the experience you've had in giving presentations, online or otherwise. The thing to always remember is that no-one's perfect, so don't worry if your experience is not as vast as it would appear that they want.

With leadership abilities, depending on the post you've applied for, they may wish to hear evidence of previous leadership strategy. If you have limited experience in this category, you can say so, but also add that you believe you would make a good job of it and give a reason. Always try to put a positive slant on anything that is unproven. If you ever get asked 'Why?' as you probably will, you will need to have an answer prepared. You will always need to justify.

For technical knowledge and special abilities, your qualifications may speak for you. However, you will be expected to converse with an up-to-date knowledge of what's going on in your field. Of course, the job you're applying for may not warrant any questions in this area.

The other areas of interest to the interviewer are almost certainly an ability to show that you have a well-developed emotional and social intelligence. They can discover this through general questioning to find out the last time you were angry or happy and why. It's always the 'why' that interests them. Even if there's something not so desirable in your history, they will be interested in the 'why', because if there's a good reason, then they are unlikely to hold anything against you, particularly if you can show that you've changed your character and attitude.

You may also find that the interviewer asks what seem to be very simple and easy-to-answer questions, and everything goes well. And I hope it does. It's just that if you prepare for really challenging questions, you will be in a much better position than the person who hasn't. It will give you an air of confidence which always goes down well in interview situations.

Defining Attributes

- Key personality characteristics
- Experience, training and technical skills
- Education and formal qualifications
- Special abilities: IT management, presentations etc.
- Mental and emotional attributes

Presenting Information

1. Use positive sentences: avoid using don't, isn't, can't, no, not, etc.
2. Use open gesture and mind your body language.
3. Avoid beginning a sentence with 'But...' or 'Yes, but...'.
4. Appear enthusiastic about your answers.
5. Ask for clarification if you are not sure.
6. Show optimism and be positive about the future.
7. Only ask a question if you are interested in hearing the answer.
8. Always turn off your phone.

'What is a date, really, but a job interview that lasts all night. The only difference between a date and a job interview is that in not many job interviews is there a chance you'll end up naked at the end of it.'

Seinfeld

Summary

Going to a job interview is a little like getting ready for a presentation, since the two key aspects apply to both: prepare and rehearse. People generally put a lot of effort into the C.V. and covering note. Unfortunately, though, as soon as they get notice of an interview, they're under the misguided notion that the decision is virtually made and all they have to do is turn up. How wrong they are. The covering letter and the C.V. are just the 'tease' to get you the interview; then the fun begins. Prepare and rehearse possible questions with a friend.

15. Online Interactions

'The way of the world is meeting people through other people'

Robert Kerrigan

Technology and the Future of Social Interaction

This chapter had to change for 2021. Technology is making what we do today redundant in a shorter space of time than ever before. It is astonishing that our lives are so incredibly tied into tech; much of it through necessity. For example, QR codes are now commonplace due to the COVID-19 situation where people are asked to 'register' at restaurants, transport, public toilets, everywhere. In some restaurants, menus no longer exist; you photo a QR code to download it.

Most people are embracing the tech. They see that an online presence is imperative to making any business a success. Influencers now exist to persuade you into buying various products, with a good living to be made from such activities. Many people now make more from advertising on their YouTube channel than they did from their regular jobs.

Online interactions will only grow in the foreseeable future. But there are my top five key perspectives to keep in mind.

It Is Not Safe

To highlight this, let me use the example of a traffic situation. I was trying to make a difficult right-hand turn in heavy traffic. I was waiting for a safe gap, but what I determined safe was too long for the car behind me to wait. The driver beeped her horn, gestured wildly and berated me for taking too long. She was angry and very confident she was in the right. However, I wasn't to be rushed into a rash decision and still waited until a larger, safer gap appeared. Again the woman beeped, but this time it was longer and angrier. I decided enough was enough and put the handbrake on, got out of the car, and walked up to her car window. As I did so, her expression changed from one of anger to surprise to shock and fear. I knocked on the window to speak to her and smiled unthreateningly. She lowered the window a little and meekly said I was taking too long. I politely said I'd pull over to let her go first. And she thanked me.

There are two points here: the first is that in a face-to-face interaction, the woman was very different to that when she felt protected behind the wheel and steel of her car and I was safely in mine. She was more herself: aggressive, rude and self-righteous. She felt 'safe' to be like that. However, that safe feeling was shattered when I got out of the car as she was unsure how I was going to react. It is highly likely she expected me to act like she would, with road rage. All of a sudden, her situation became very unsafe. The fact that I reacted in an emotionally intelligent manner brought her great relief. In terms of interacting online, people feel 'safe' when they write things in their house or a place they feel comfortable and they write things on social media which they think will only be read by the intended recipients and no-one else. And because it appears 'safe', people will reveal their innermost thoughts and plans. Such people will post items on social media assuming that they will have everyone think the same. Many will, and many will not. Like the angry driver, who thinks that because she drives a particular way, she expects everyone else to do the same as her. Yet, many people will not. There will be those who get angry and 'Troll' the person, which can lead to a whole host of worrying scenarios.

1. Cancel Culture

There are a lot of people who look for other people to disagree with and pick an online fight: to cancel you and your point of view. Yes, there are encouraging and altruistic people too, but just be aware. there are so many nasty comments on social media from people who are convinced they know better. They think they know a lot about something and if they repeat it often enough it becomes a fact (to them), and then they defend their knowledge with their emotions. It's a case of shallow personality since they tie all their emotions into these exchanges. And to what end? What's the purpose? To feel vindicated that they were right in the first place (if they ever were)? So you can see that, like most things in the real world, the cyber world also has its fair share of problems. And this leads to the perpetuation of myths, legends and fake news. On the surface, there's nothing much wrong with this. After all, most histories are based on myths and legends. However, at a deeper level there are people who live for these conspiracy theories and want to believe them so badly that they blur the line between fact and fiction.

2. The Truth and Fake News

Perhaps the best example of this is the way Donald Trump used the phrase 'Fake News' to describe much information coming from the American media when he didn't agree with it. Another example is during the Covid 19 lockdown, frightful messages of doom and gloom were forwarded on WhatsApp so many times that the App's algorithms limited the number of people you could forward them to. The same applied to funny videos too, just to put things into perspective. And many of these messages appeared so real it was almost impossible to think of them as fake. But a lot of them were. There is a very reliable adage which states 'If it seems unbelievable, it probably is' - even if you have visual evidence to the contrary. And it's instantaneous. People forward without really thinking.

Online selling is a good example of this. Most businesses are already very well aware that the best form of marketing is word of mouth, and with social media, that just got a whole lot more important. people are now paid to use their friends to make money with false feedback reports and advertising such as 'I was shocked at what a good product it was so you might like to check them out at www.blahblahblah.com so you can see for yourself how good they are.' The writing is insincere, the message is scripted, and it's just one step removed from multilevel marketing or a pyramid scheme. Simply be aware that the 'Influencer's job is to get you to buy, they only care about people if there's a risk of a significant number of people unsubscribing resulting in a loss of advertising revenue for the 'Influencer'.

3. Nothing is Private

A picture may paint a thousand words, but a video is the whole book. Because the majority of the world's population processes information at a primarily visual level, people can access information of their choice. But is it really their choice? I'm sure you've noticed that you will be bombarded by hotel advertising if you look at a holiday destination. You may be under the impression you've turned off all the cookie access, but your information **can** be accessed, particularly if you are not careful over the settings you choose. Using a 'Tor' or 'Onion' search engine is no guarantee of privacy either. If it's online, it can be accessed by other people who are not the intended recipients.

As with emails, once you press 'send', you have little or no control over what happens to that information. In fact, people are hired by recruitment firms to check the social media pages of potential hires. It really is quite extraordinary that people are happy to post the most ridiculous pictures of themselves on their Facebook and other social media pages with the idea that only their friends can see them. As with most everything else in cyberspace, if you can upload it, then someone else can download it. What if those photos were posted to the recruiting officer just before your job interview? What if that joke you posted online was sent to your future mother-in-law the day before your wedding? What if....

It's a powerful tool to influence people's decision making, often without them being consciously aware they have been influenced. There is an extraordinary amount of information on you in cyberspace.

4. Addiction

Social media is addictive. Think about a soap opera you used to be a fan of. How did you feel if you thought you were going to miss an episode? Did you ever play Candy Crush or Farmville? How did you feel if you didn't get your daily dose of the App? Do you worry about how many followers you have or how many Likes you get?

Human beings are social animals. We need the contact, but this can all get out of hand. Apps, YouTube channels and pretty much all social media is out to get you addicted to their site. It's all to do with revenue from advertisements (or influence). Remember, they care about the money much more than they care about you. You help create their wealth.

Political or club affiliations also exploit the addictive nature of social media. Countries and political entities have been trying to influence you for a long time via their news channels, but now they can influence you directly. Their presence on social media is vast. The various sites will lure you in with slick productions and such realistic content. Look at how Al Qaeda, the Islamic state and other militant organisations have managed to convince people to commit heinous crimes. People become addicted to something which helps their self-esteem and helps them feel relevant in this brave new world. Then they are encouraged to act on it. And I bet you think you would never fall for such a thing. Well, so did most of the people who became addicted. Is there a programme or an App which you couldn't go a week without checking?

Zoom, MS Teams, and Other Business Tools

Tech development has grown exponentially. It is now relatively easy to get information to large groups of people fast. The Covid 19 pandemic has forced many of us to work from home and pushed us into learning new online skills. Zoom - and other online software - meetings have become commonplace. School classes and management training have had to adapt and adopt. Even when the pandemic has been tamed or we have all been vaccinated against it, it is highly likely that online meetings and training will remain a key feature of future work. The advantages are greater.

Information is instantaneous. Could any business survive today without the use of a mobile phone? I doubt it. As a result, we should get used to the way tech is shaping our lives and adapt and adopt to be successful. The following are my top ten golden guidelines to ensure you interact as effectively as possible.

1. **There's STILL No Such Thing as a Free Lunch.**

   Nothing is free. There is always a cost attached, whether it's your time, influence, money, personal details etc. Scams abound. In the past they were fairly simple and along the lines of 'Nigerian Princess needs you to help with her fortune'. These days, they can appear so genuine and real. If someone is offering you something, an exclusive opportunity, do a background check first. If anything appears like a bargain, there is a good reason why. Find out what it is. Or better, just delete.

2. **Don't Drink and Tweet.**

   Have you ever woken up the next day after that extra glass of wine and checked the messages you sent the previous evening when they all seemed so poignant and funny? Yes, we've all been there. This advice relates to all forms of online interaction, especially shopping. Just don't.

3. **Be Security Minded.**

   It may be in your nature to trust people, to give them the benefit of the doubt. It's a great thing face-to-face, but not online. There are literally hundreds of thousands of people who want to get their hands on your data and information. They will send you PayPal or Bank emails saying your accounts are locked due to suspicious activity and they require you to input your data. Don't do it. Use your social media sites' password generator. Yes, I know it's impossible to remember it, but that's partly the point. It's designed to be hacker proof. Use extra authentication security steps if they're offered. It may be an extra step before you access the site you want, but it will be worth it.

4. **Be Emotionally and Socially Intelligent.**

   This applies even more so to online interactions. People feel safer online like the angry woman in the story at the beginning of the chapter. They write things they would never have the courage to say to your face. Do not rise to the bait. Keep calm and click cancel.

5. **What Animal are You?**

   There are thousands of (interesting) quizzes out there tempting you to 'Find out…' Avoid them! They are there to mine you for your data. There will be a question such as 'Do you allow XYZ App to access your photos, address book and other data?' Do not give permission. This information is then used to create an online profile which is sold on to advertisers to target you with specific ads.

6. **Post Online Like it was the Office Noticeboard.**

   The photo you posted of yourself at the Christmas party around your friend's house where you let your hair down is now a bit of an embarrassment, so you delete it from your 'photos'. Not so much harm done, you think. But there will be another copy of it somewhere in cyberspace. Holiday pics? Send them after you return. Burglars love holiday pics.

7. **Do It Now.**

If you have an idea to use social media as your platform to sell a product or service, then get it out there as soon as possible before someone else does. Procrastination is the death knell of success.

8. **The Easy Buck.**

Following on from # 7, setting up an online business is challenging even if you have the IT skills necessary. Those who say they made a fortune online usually miss the bit about the hard work which is essential for success. Success comes with hours of input and much thought. You need to love what you do. Then, listen to your customers' and friends' comments, especially the tough ones. Diversify then try again.

9. **Social Media is not Work.**

It can be, but if you upload content for free without a long-term plan as to how it will generate an income, then it's not work.

10. Market.

Simply being online does not guarantee you will amass a huge number of followers. If anything, the algorithms are skewed against new sites. You do need to have great content which is interesting, new, informative and updated regularly. It's hard work. You can also opt to pay to advertise your site/product through the main channels.

'Oh brave new world, where mothers don't ask their children how their day was. Facebook and Twitter answered for them.'

Timothy Correa

16. The Final Piece of the Communication Jigsaw

'Denying desire is to take away the potential of someone who could have had a future.'

David Hirst

Willingness

There is one final thing to communicate with anyone which, in many ways, governs all of the previous chapters: willingness. This is the final piece in the jigsaw of communication, for without willingness there will be very little improvement. You need to have the willingness to try new things out, and willingness to step outside your comfort zone to learn new skills and behaviours. There also needs to be a willingness to trust other people and take measured risks with them.

Without willingness there will be very little improvement.

Imagine you have been on a course to learn parachuting - yes, I wouldn't do this in reality either - and during the course you made some excellent friends as you were all put in moderately stressful situations together. However, you came to dislike one of your instructors and even had a heated argument at one stage as you sensed that he was picking on you and somehow had it in for you all the time. Then in the plane on the day of your first real jump, another parachutist informs you that this particular instructor had packed your parachute personally. And then comes the time to jump, but would you?

You see, to change the situation, we first have to change ourselves and that requires a willingness to do so. We should take a little time to reflect on why we have certain perceptions, views and biases. From this reflection we are able to get a better picture of the person we'd like to be. The 'how to get there' is described in all the previous chapters, but the willingness to do so still remains. Let's face it, we see the world as we are conditioned to see it. Some people like to believe that we are who we are because we are the genetic products of our parents. 'You are your mother's daughter; you are your father's son', and so on. While I understand that there's a lot of evidence to support this theory, I think there's more to it. Another theory is that you are a product of your psychological development – your exposure to information. Again, I see that there's quite a lot of truth in this. Finally, there are those who see a person's development mostly as a product of their environment – we respond to that which is around us. Actually, there is truth in all of these theories, but the one crucial aspect of them all is the concept of 'choice'.

To change the situation, we first have to change ourselves and that requires a willingness to do so.

Irrespective of the influences we have, we always have an element of choice. Granted, it may not seem like much of a choice sometimes, for example your boss telling you to finish the report by Friday or start looking for another job. But it's still a choice. The notion of choice is important because it gives you power over the direction of your life.

Irrespective of the influences we have, we always have the element of choice.

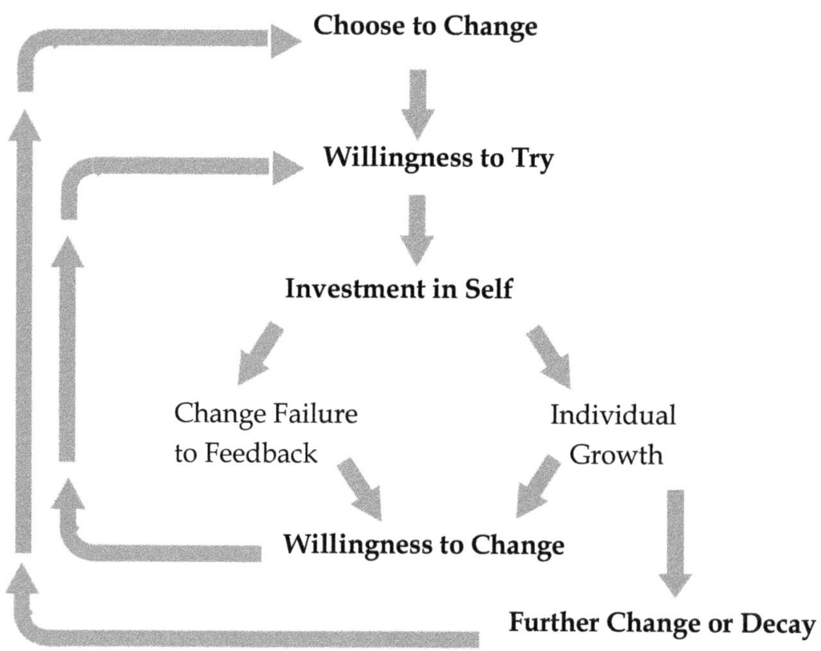

Without constant exposure to new information or experiences, will result in a state of decay. New experiences allow you to see the world differently, and if you perceive things differently, you will feel differently and therefore behave differently.

Different perceptions lead to different behaviours i.e. the new and more effective you. The only thing holding you back is the willingness to try. And I fully understand the hesitance. It's a little like going for a yearly medical or dental check-up. People avoid the doctor or dentist precisely for the same reason that they should go in the first place i.e. they are frightened they might find something wrong with them that needs fixing. Yet, after you have been, there's this tremendous sense of relief that you've finally overcome your fear and the unknown (the real fear) is now known and you can get on with your life. If you need a tooth fixing or you need to change your diet or take anti-cholesterol pills, then so be it. But the fear will have gone. Then you can look back and wonder what all the fuss was about and why you had put it off for so long. You then promise yourself that you won't wait so long for the next check-up.

Without doubt, the desire to change is worth a thousand teachers.

Sometimes the willingness to change comes from another person. It could be your boss telling you that you need to become more effective in the workplace or you can kiss the chances of promotion goodbye. It could come from your partner by them saying that if you don't start changing, they will leave you. A bit drastic, perhaps, but I think you get the picture. The impetus for change may come from a number of different places, but the main issue is the desire to be a more effective communicator than you currently are. Without doubt, the desire to change is worth a thousand teachers.

I have often heard people complain about the corruption in their respective countries, particularly in Asia. But my take on this is that nearly all governments are corrupt, it's just that some are cleverer at covering it up. Likewise, some people appear fearless and willing to try all manner of things. However, they too are also fearful of the unknown, everyone is. It's what gives people the adrenalin rush when they go parachuting, for example. It's just that they too are better at covering it up.

And when people complain to you about the lack of fun in their lives and seem persistent in wanting to bring you down to their level too, just refund their misery and get on with achieving the life **you** want. Go on, take a chance. Oh, and by the way, think about buying a lottery ticket. You may win. If you don't buy one, you will never win. Take a chance and work on some of the skills detailed in this book, and unlike the lottery, your chances of winning are almost certain. Begin today.

'Today is the yesterday you'll wish for tomorrow.'

David Hirst

Summary

From making a good first impression to being more effective in meetings, negotiations, and at speaking in public, this book has all you need to become the best you can be, and more of the person you want to be. The simple fact that you're reading this indicates that you have the desire to change which is the starting point, so take a measured risk and put the skills covered in the previous chapters into practice. Follow the Golden Guidelines and see the changes they effect. Remember, the memories you so fondly treasure are borne in the moments of today. And besides, life's just too short not to try, isn't it?

www.ingramcontent.com/pod-product-compliance
Ingram Content Group UK Ltd.
Pitfield, Milton Keynes, MK11 3LW, UK
UKHW022027190726
13853UKWH00005B/2147